THE CATHAR WAY

A WALKER'S GUIDE TO THE SENTIER CATHARE,
A TRAIL LINKING CATHAR CASTLES
IN SOUTHERN FRANCE

About the Author

Alan Mattingly was director of the Ramblers' Association in Great Britain from 1974 to 1998. At various times during that period, he also held other posts in the outdoor and conservation movements, including that of chairman of the Council for National Parks.

A member of the Outdoor Writers' Guild, he received that organisation's Golden Eagle Award in 1998. He is also a recipient of the John Hunt Award (from the Countrywide Holidays Association) and the Wildlife and Countryside Link Award. His previous publications include *Tackle Rambling* (1981), *Walking in the National Parks* (1982) and *Walking in the Cathar Region* (Cicerone, 2005).

He is now based in a small town in the eastern Pyrenees that lies just below the 9000 foot (2800 metres) Pic du Canigou. When not exploring on foot that most impressive and captivating of mountains, he teaches English and writes.

THE CATHAR WAY

A WALKER'S GUIDE TO THE SENTIER CATHARE, A TRAIL LINKING CATHAR CASTLES IN SOUTHERN FRANCE

by
Alan Mattingly

2 POLICE SQUARE, MILNTHORPE, CUMBRIA LA7 7PY
www.cicerone.co.uk

First edition 2006
ISBN-10: 1 85284 486 8
ISBN-13: 978 1 85284 486 8

Photos: Alan Mattingly (unless otherwise acknowledged)
A catalogue record for this book is available from the British Library

Acknowledgements

My gratitude is due to all those, volunteers and professionals alike, who have planned, created, waymarked, maintained and written about the Sentier Cathare.

For their various measures of help, advice and patient tolerance during the writing of this book, I would also like to thank in particular: Branton Bamford, Hazel Clarke, Bernard Diamant, Lolin Jones, David Monnet, Mary Whitney and Jonathan Williams.

I am especially grateful to Wendy Mattingly, to whom this book is dedicated – she saw a great deal of the Sentier Cathare and its surrounding countryside during its writing. Not only did she not complain while the author took innumerable pictures of waymarks and signposts, conversed boringly with his dictaphone and paused often to inspect grocery stores, water taps, sanitary facilities and noticeboards, she also offered the unsolicited comment that the Sentier Cathare is a particularly fascinating and beautiful path to walk along. That is a good recommendation, because she is an excellent judge of these things and, had her opinion been otherwise, she would certainly have said so.

My future gratitude will be extended to all readers who follow all or part of the Sentier Cathare and, on finding any problems or changes to the route, inform me of them. Please send this information to the publisher by e-mail or otherwise.

Advice to Readers

Readers are advised that while every effort is taken by the author to ensure the accuracy of this guidebook, changes can occur which may affect the contents. It is advisable to check locally on transport, accommodation, shops, etc, but even rights of way can be altered. The publisher would welcome notes of any such changes.

Front cover: The town of Foix, dominated by its medieval Cathar castle, at the western end of the Sentier Cathare

CONTENTS

APPENDICES

Route Map Key

══════D27══════	principal road
══════A9══════	motorway *(autoroute)*
••••••••••••••••••••••••	Sentier Cathare (Main Route)
··································	Sentier Cathare (North Variant)
··································	Sentier Cathare (other alternative route)
1	numbered points on trail, referred to in the text (with height in metres)
- - - - - - - - - - - - - - - -	path, track or lane
┼┼┼┼┼┼┼┼┼┼┼┼┼┼┼┼┼┼┼┼┼	railway
←——←——←——←	power line
⌒⊓⊓⊓⊓⌒	crag or cliff
●	city, town, village
♜	castle (or castle ruin)
✖	wind turbine
⬆	hut, cabin
◁	lagoon, lake, pond
•	spot height (with height in metres)
■	building or ruin
✳	man-made feature
✳	special natural feature
⚲	chapel
P	parking

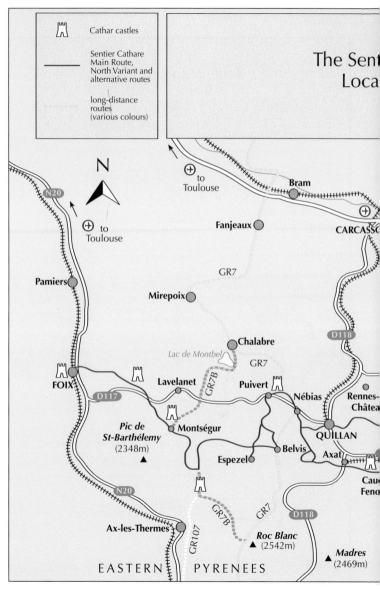

Cathar castles

Sentier Cathare
Main Route,
North Variant and
alternative routes

long-distance
routes
(various colours)

The Sent
Loca

N

⊕ to
Toulouse

⊕ to
Toulouse

N20

Bram

Fanjeaux

CARCASSO

GR7

Pamiers

Mirepoix

D118

Chalabre

Lac de Montbel

GR7

FOIX

D117

Lavelanet

GR7B

Puivert

Nébias

Rennes-
Châtea

Pic de
St-Barthélemy
(2348m)
▲

Montségur

Espezel

Belvis

QUILLAN

Axat

Cau
Feno

N20

Ax-les-Thermes

GR107

GR7B

GR7

D118

Roc Blanc
▲ (2542m)

Madres
▲ (2469m)

EASTERN   PYRENEES

8

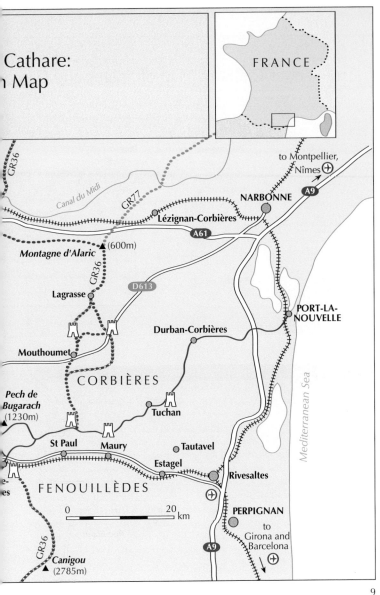

Cathare:
Map

FRANCE

to Montpellier,
Nîmes

GR36

Canal du Midi

GR77

NARBONNE

A9

Lézignan-Corbières

A61

Montagne d'Alaric (600m)

GR36

D613

PORT-LA-
NOUVELLE

Lagrasse

Durban-Corbières

Mouthoumet

CORBIÈRES

Mediterranean Sea

Pech de
Bugarach
(1230m)

Tuchan

St Paul   Maury

Tautavel

Estagel

Rivesaltes

FENOUILLÈDES

0   20 km

PERPIGNAN

to
Girona and
Barcelona

A9

GR36

Canigou
(2785m)

The Sentier Cathare: Map of Stages and Cathar

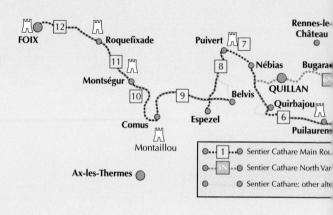

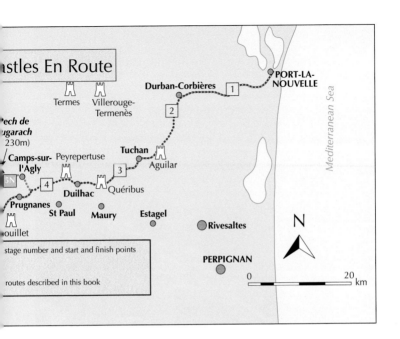

astles En Route

Termes   Villerouge-
              Termenès

Durban-Corbières ☐1   PORT-LA-
                                          NOUVELLE

Pech de
ugarach
(1230m)   ☐2

Camps-sur- Peyrepertuse   Tuchan
l'Agly   Aguilar
                                    ☐3

SN   ☐4   Duilhac   Quéribus
Prugnanes   St Paul   Maury   Estagel
ouillet   ● Rivesaltes

stage number and start and finish points

routes described in this book

● Rivesaltes

PERPIGNAN
●

N

0   20
|___|___|___|___|___| km

Mediterranean Sea

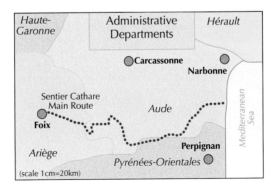

Haute-   Administrative   Hérault
Garonne   Departments

                    ● Carcassonne   ●
                                    Narbonne

Sentier Cathare
Main Route   Aude
●
Foix

Ariège   Perpignan
          Pyrénées-Orientales ●

(scale 1cm=20km)

Mediterranean Sea

11

Peyrepertuse Castle, on Stage 4 of the trail; an enormous and impregnable fortress, it was one of the last of the Cathars' refuges to fall to the invading French army

INTRODUCTION

THE SENTIER CATHARE

*'the most celebrated
footpath in France'*

The Sentier Cathare – or Cathar Way – is a trail of discovery in the Languedoc region of southern France, leading walkers from one famous Cathar castle to another. In its 250-kilometre westward passage from the Mediterranean coastline to the Ariège capital of Foix, the trail links nine of these legendary fortresses.

The 'Cathar castles' are mostly perched on high, rocky pinnacles. They gave refuge to followers of a 13th-century sect of heretical Christians – the Languedoc Cathars. The Cathars were brutally crushed during a ruthless 'crusade' launched against them by the Catholic Church and the French kingdom, and their rise and fall deeply affected the course of western Europe's history.

After centuries of neglect and decay, the Cathar castles are today being carefully restored. They arouse great fascination among people from all over the world, including those travelling on foot. Indeed, a noticeboard by the village square in Nébias, about halfway along the trail, proclaims that the Sentier Cathare is 'the most celebrated footpath in France'.

Now that is quite a bold claim to make, yet the Sentier Cathare is without doubt very popular, and whether or not it is *the* most celebrated trail in France, it is certainly one of the best-conceived and best-maintained walking routes that I have ever encountered, for which its instigators (who include the Mayor of Nébias, Louis Salavy) and present-day caretakers are to be congratulated.

As well as a trail of discovery of the Cathar castles, the Sentier Cathare is also a long hill walk. It rises and falls along its full extent, climbing from sea level to over 1300 metres, often following ancient inter-village footpaths. The countryside it passes through includes remote plateaux, deep valleys and gorges, meadows, forests, vineyards, towering cliffs and wildflower-rich upland pastures. The trail generally follows the grain of the land, over limestone hills that run parallel with the Pyrenees, whose snow-capped peaks form an almost constantly present horizon to the south.

In landscapes such as these, in fine weather, the good-to-be-alive feeling that walking in the outdoors offers can be at its zenith. But in passing through the land where the Cathar heresy flourished and was suppressed, the Sentier Cathare also offers a thought-provoking history lesson. My earlier guidebook, *Walking in*

13

Nébias, a welcome resting place on Stage 7 of the Sentier Cathare

the Cathar Region (Cicerone, 2005), concluded with a few reflections on the history of the Cathars, and its possible lessons for present-day Europe and beyond. Overall, I agree with the sentiments expressed by Joseph Ribas, who writes with passion and initimate knowledge of the Pyrenees and the Pays Cathare. Ribas wrote, *'Les coquelicots refleurissent sur les champs de bataille et, avec eux, reviennent les vendanges et les moissons. On n'étouffe pas dans le sang la volonté d'une fleur.'* In short, and inadequately translated, this says that where there was once bloody conflict, there are now flowers and wine harvests, which is certainly true of the Cathar region, so we have some grounds for drawing an optimistic conclusion from the Cathars' otherwise less than cheerful story.

I would urge anyone who is thinking of visiting the region to read about the history of the Cathars. Whether you conclude that they were martyred saints or credulous fanatics, you will surely find their story poignant, and be fired by a desire to explore the countryside and the monuments in which their drama was played out.

David Monnet, based in the Carcassonne headquarters of the Aude département, is one of the Sentier Cathare's principal 'caretakers'

A trek along the Sentier Cathare is the perfect way to conduct such an exploration.

THE CATHARS

The term 'Cathar' was not used themselves by the followers of this faith, rather, it was applied by the Catholic Church to this particular group of heretics. It may originally have been a term of offence, meaning cat-lover – that is, a sorcerer or witch – but the Cathars called themselves simply Christians. The Cathar 'priests' – of which there were women as well as men – were referred to by their Catholic opponents as 'Perfects', meaning perfect (i.e. complete) heretics, but their followers just called them 'good Christians', or '**Bons Hommes**' and '**Bonnes Femmes**'.

However, they were Christians who denied the authority of the Pope and had profound theological differences with the Catholic Church. In particular, they had a belief – **dualism** – that good and evil spring from different sources. They regarded the material world as plainly evil, and concluded that it could not have been created by the God of the Bible. Such a belief was totally at odds with Catholic doctrine, and indeed, the Cathars even saw the Catholic Church itself as the work of the devil. The broadcasting of such an opinion was not a good strategy for making friends and influencing people in the heretic-burning years of medieval Europe.

The Cathars were based over a much wider area than that covered by the Location Map on pages 8 and 9. In fact they were numerous in several parts of western Europe, including northern Italy and the Rhineland. However, from the 11th century they established especially deep roots in Languedoc.

The Bons Hommes and Bonnes Femmes who preached Catharism were ascetic. They worked in the community as, for example, craftsmen, preached in a language that everyone could understand, and levied no taxes – not surprisingly, they were popular with the independent-minded people of Languedoc. In addition, the region's 'nobility' (i.e. its warlords) protected them –

15

The trail was designed to connect several medieval castles linked to the Cathars, and most of them are hilltop fortresses offering marvellous panoramas; this is the view from Castel Sabordas to Château St Pierre (the so-called Fenouillet castles, Stage 5, Main Route) – in the background, the Pech de Bugarach

indeed, many members of 'noble' families in Languedoc were themselves Cathars.

The Catholic Church could not but see the Cathars as a threat to its very existence, and the French crown, whose territory at that time was confined to the northern part of what is now France, became eager to take possession of Languedoc. These two irresistible forces, church and crown,

together met head-on the immovable object of the Cathar faith, and jointly launched against the Cathars a crusade that was just as cruel and bloody as those dispatched to 'save' the Holy Land.

What happened next – and in subsequent centuries – is summarised in the following chronology. (Cathar castles that you will encounter along the Sentier Cathare are highlighted.)

1208 Pope Innocent III calls for a crusade against the Cathars of Languedoc.

July 1209 Led by French forces, the huge army of what became known as the 'Albigensian Crusade' besieges Béziers. In July, the town's walls are breached, the town is sacked and thousands of its inhabitants, both Cathars and Catholics, are massacred.

August 1209 The crusaders' army seizes Carcassonne. Simon de Montfort, a brilliant but pitiless military commander, is appointed to lead the crusade.

1210 De Montfort attacks and takes control of several castles where Cathars and their sympathisers are taking refuge, executing Cathars and torturing and massacring anyone who shows resistance to his forces. In particular, Termes Castle, in the Corbières region, falls to de Montfort. **Aguilar Castle** (Stage 2 of the Sentier Cathare), which belongs to the Cathar family who owned Termes, is then also taken by de Montfort, without resistance. **Puivert Castle** (Stage 7), also owned by a Cathar family, is another fortress that is seized by the crusaders' army.

1213 The crusaders' army wins a decisive victory at the Battle of Muret (near Toulouse). The King of Aragon, who had come to the aid of the Languedoc barons, is killed in this battle.

1215 **Foix Castle** (Stage 12), for long a major stronghold of resistance to de Montfort, surrenders.

1218 Simon de Montfort is killed in a skirmish outside Toulouse. During the following years the Languedoc barons regain many of their previous possessions, and the strength of the Cathars is restored.

1226 The French king, Louis VIII, relaunches the crusade, with overwhelming force.

1229 The Count of Toulouse, Languedoc's principal defender, concedes defeat to the French crown. He signs the Treaty of Paris, which leads to Languedoc being absorbed into the French kingdom, but many people in Languedoc remain true to the Cathar faith.

1233 Pope Gregory IX launches the Inquisition in Languedoc. Its hated agents terrorise the local population, and their methods prove effective in wearing away support for Catharism.

1240 Various dispossessed Languedoc barons make an audacious attempt to recover Carcassonne from the French, and Guilhem de Peyrepertuse is one of their supporters. The attempt fails and the conspirators flee south, pursued by French troops. **Peyrepertuse Castle** (Stage 4) is besieged, and eventually Guilhem surrenders it to the French.

1242 Agents of the Inquisition are murdered in Avignonet by Cathar knights from Montségur.

1243–44 Montségur Castle (Stage 11), the most famous of the Cathar strongholds, is besieged and then taken by French forces. In March 1244 over 200 Cathars are burnt at the stake below the castle.

1255 Quéribus Castle (Stage 3), said to be the last bastion of the Cathars, is finally taken by the French.

1258 The Treaty of Corbeil is signed. This agreement between the kings of France and Aragon establishes a clear frontier between the two kingdoms. At the same time, or not long afterwards, a number of former Cathar strongholds along or near this frontier come under the firm control of the French king, including the **Fenouillet** castles (Stage 5, Main Route) and **Roquefixade Castle** (Stage 12). Several of these castles are rebuilt or substantially strengthened to defend France's new southern frontier, including **Puilaurens Castle** (Stage 6, Main Route).

1299 In the mountains of Ariège around Ax-les-Thermes there is a Cathar revival led by Peter Autier. It enjoys widespread support, but is eventually crushed. Autier is burnt at the stake in Toulouse in 1310.

1317 Jacques Fournier, Bishop of Pamiers (and later Pope Benoît XII) begins Inquisitorial hearings into the activities of presumed Cathar supporters in the village of Montaillou (near Comus, Stage 10). Some of the records of these hearings have survived, and they reveal a remarkably detailed picture of life in this medieval Cathar village.

1321 Guillaume Bélibaste, the last of the Languedoc Bons Hommes, is burnt at the stake in Villerouge-Termenès Castle, in the Corbières region. Originally from Cubières-sur-Cinoble (Stage 4, North Variant), Bélibaste had led a small community of Cathars who had taken refuge in Catalonia.

1659 The Pyrenees Treaty, between France and Spain, is signed, with the result that the frontier between the two countries moves south, to its present line. As a result, several of the Cathar castles that had defended the former frontier since 1258 (and which today lie along the Sentier Cathare) lose their military significance, and are either dismantled, or abandoned and left to fall into ruin.

1891 Bérenger Saunière, the priest of Rennes-le-Château (visible from Stage 6, North Variant), discovers a hidden tomb in his village church. From about this date, he mysteriously acquires a good deal of wealth and spends most of it on the church and other nearby buildings. One of many theories about the origin of Saunière's wealth is that he discovered treasure hidden by Cathars who had managed to escape from Montségur while the castle was under siege in the winter of 1243–4.

CATHAR CASTLES

The so-called **Cathar castles** are medieval fortifications (or, more often, just the remains of them) located in places where the Cathars lived, preached or sought refuge. Many of these fortifications were built on vertiginous cliffs, crags or steep-sided pinnacles. They are striking in appearance and loaded with sombre history and mystery.

As described in the above chronology, after the **Albigensian Crusade** the French reconstructed several of the castles in which the Cathars had once taken refuge, then, in the 17th century, when the castles lost their strategic importance, most of them decayed, the 'castles in the sky', which have since become symbols of the Cathar faith and its demise, being bequeathed to posterity. These sometimes romantic, sometimes forbidding castles became the focus of fantastic fables and, in our time, tourist attractions of international repute.

The citadels as we see them today would have been mostly unrecognisable to the Cathars. Little is known about how most of them looked when the Cathars inhabited them, but they are located on sites that undoubtedly have strong historical connections with the Cathars, so 'Cathar castles' is a perfectly reasonable title for them.

THE CATHAR REGION

The area referred to in this book as '**Cathar castle country**', or the '**Cathar region**', is the area shown on the Location Map on pages 8 and 9, and most of the best known and most striking of the Cathar castles are situated here.

The Cathar region is in **Languedoc**, this name deriving from the language that was spoken by the area's inhabitants (the *langue d'oc* – see below). In medieval times Languedoc was not a single administrative unit, rather, its unity was based principally upon its language. The main city was Toulouse, and Languedoc extended north towards the Dordogne, east towards the Rhône valley and south towards the Pyrenees.

Invaded and occupied successively by the Romans, Visigoths, Moors and Franks, in the 10th century Languedoc was divided up into feudal principalities. At that time, those principalities were not part of the French kingdom, and the biggest of them was the domain of the Count of Toulouse. Languedoc became part of the French kingdom in the 13th century.

Today, the name Languedoc survives in the title of the administrative region known as Languedoc–Roussillon, a region covering the administrative departments of Aude, Gard, Hérault, Lozère and the Pyrénées-Orientales. It is smaller than medieval Languedoc.

The **langue d'oc** was a collection of Roman dialects spoken in much of what is now southern France, in contrast to the *langue d'oïl*, the collection of Roman dialects that was spoken in the northern half of France, and which formed the basis of the French language. The term *langue d'oc* is synonymous with **'Occitan'**, and was a major language of culture in the Middle Ages, enjoying a renaissance in the 19th century that has continued until our own time. Occitan is also used as an adjective, meaning of or from the area within which the Occitan language is spoken.

In Cathar castle country **'Pays Cathare'** ('Cathar country') signs are seen regularly along the way. The Pays Cathare logo was developed by the departments of Ariège, Aude and Hérault, and is used widely in the region, including on some signposts along the Sentier Cathare. This curious emblem apparently depicts the sun (or maybe the moon) rising above the land below, representing the influence that the Cathar religion radiated over this country. The division of the sun/moon into a black sector and a white sector represents the dualism of the Cathar faith, and the scribbled appearance of the motif is said to denote the wounds that were inflicted on the region by the painful events of the crusade against the Cathars. The slightly irregular line underneath represents the hilly, sometimes mountainous nature of the terrain.

THE SENTIER CATHARE – PORT-LA-NOUVELLE TO FOIX

Origin and Character of the Trail

The Sentier Cathare runs for about 250km from **Port-la-Nouvelle** to **Foix** across hilly, tranquil French countryside where, in between the occasional villages and Cathar castles, there is often little sign of human habitation. The waymarked trail follows ancient footpaths and contemporary jeep tracks and forest roads.

The curious 'Pays Cathare' logo appears on many Sentier Cathare waymark posts, as here on Stage 7

The Sentier Cathare was traced out in the latter part of the 20th century – a modern creation inspired by events that happened some 800 years ago. Like many other long-distance paths, it was essentially a product of two things: walkers' enthusiasm and the tourist industry's recognition that hikers' trails bring rural prosperity. What was unique in the design of this trail was its association with the most famous group of hilltop fortresses in Europe, for, en route, the Sentier Cathare passes by nine Cathar castles, namely **Aguilar**, **Quéribus**, **Peyrepertuse**, **Fenouillet**, **Puilaurens**, **Puivert**, **Montségur**, **Roquefixade** and **Foix**.

Most Sentier Cathare walkers will probably start from Port-la-Nouvelle on the Mediterranean coast and head west to the bustling regional town of Foix in the Ariège Valley. This is perhaps the more satisfying direction to take, as two of the main highlights of the walk – Montségur and Foix castles – are saved until towards the end. The Sentier Cathare is not as demanding as mountain trails like the trans-Pyrenean GR10, but it is moderately tough and should not be underestimated.

The trail is conventionally divided into 12 stages (see Route Summary Table, page 37). From Stage 4 to Stage 7 there is a southern route (called the **Main Route** in this book) and a **North Variant**, both of which are described here. The trail is used by horse riders and cyclists, as well as walkers.

Appendix 3 covers other long-distance paths in the Cathar region – in particular, certain national long-distance routes, or GR paths ('Sentiers de Grande Randonnée'), which are waymarked with small red and white painted rectangles. These are shown on the Location Map on pages 8 and 9. The Sentier Cathare is not, at the time of writing, classified as a GR path, but it is very well maintained.

Waymarking and Route-finding

The Sentier Cathare is well waymarked throughout its length, but at the time of writing the system of waymarking varies along the trail. From its eastern end at Port-la-Nouvelle, to a point on Stage 10 just beyond Comus, most of the Sentier Cathare is in the administrative *département* of **Aude** (parts of Stages 4 and 5 are in the **Pyrénées-Orientales** *département* – the P-O). The rest of the route, to its western end in Foix, is in **Ariège**.

In Aude and the P-O, the trail (both the Main Route and the North Variant) is indicated by blue and yellow (supposedly ochre) waymarks. In the Ariège region the waymarks are red and yellow.

The blue and yellow waymarks along the trail in Aude and the P-O continue to appear even where the trail coincides with a GR path (i.e. the GR path's red and white waymarks are also present). In Ariège, however, red and white waymarks are generally the only ones to be seen where the

From Stage 1 to Stage 10, the route of the Sentier Cathare is indicated by blue and yellow waymarks like this one (the orange disk indicates that this part of the trail is also suitable for horse riders)…

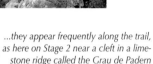

…they appear frequently along the trail, as here on Stage 2 near a cleft in a limestone ridge called the Grau de Padern

Sometimes the waymarks tell you to turn left or (as here) right…

…and sometimes they tell you not to go down the path directly ahead

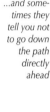

The basic waymarks are supplemented along the way with signposts, some of which, like this one, carry a sketch of the route ahead

Other signposts, like this one in Quillan, tell you when the walkers' route goes one way (here, to the left) and the route for horse riders goes another way (here, to the right)

From Stage 10 to Stage 12, in the Ariège département, the trail is indicated by different types of signs (like this one) and by red and yellow waymarks

Sentier Cathare coincides with the route of a GR path (i.e. the red and yellow ones tend to disappear).

At various points along the trail, especially at the beginning and end of each stage, you will see, in addition to the Sentier Cathare waymarks and signposts, schematic maps indicating where you are in relation to principal locations en route.

Additional waymarks in the form of orange discs or bands also appear from time to time, indicating where the trail can be followed by horse riders. On some stages, alternative routes for horse riders are signposted, and these carry orange-only waymarks. A few such alternatives are described in this book where they are of particular interest to walkers, but for the most part they are not described in detail here.

Along the way you will often see other path waymarks, including yellow ones for local walking routes that cross or coincide with the Sentier Cathare, but despite what you might imagine, all this creates hardly any confusion. The Sentier Cathare is so well used and carries so many signposts and waymarks that, as long as you keep your eyes open for those signposts and waymarks, you will only occasionally need to refer to a map or the route description in this book. The main purpose of the route description is to reassure you that you are on the right route, and to give special guidance where particular care is needed.

Along the Sentier Cathare many other, usually unwaymarked, paths and tracks turn off the waymarked route. Few of these turnings are mentioned in my route description, because they are just too numerous. However, to daydreaming walkers like your humble author, they offer manifold opportunities for wandering off the trail by mistake – please don't copy his errors and get lost in the forest.

Normally it is obvious which turning you should take to keep on the Sentier Cathare, but if in doubt – because, for example, of an absence of waymarking at a certain point – a good general rule is as follows: because the Sentier Cathare is now so well used, the turning you want is probably the path or track which seems to be the more heavily used. Follow that one, and if you do not see a Sentier Cathare waymark within 10 or 15 minutes, go back to the turning and try the other. However, where the Sentier Cathare itself divides into alternative routes, both alternatives will carry Sentier Cathare waymarks, so take special care to be sure to select the route you want.

In general, whether or not you are conscious of having recently turned off at a fork or crossing, if you walk for more than about 15 minutes without seeing a Sentier Cathare waymark, it would be wise to go back to the last point where you *did* see one, and check your route.

Changes to the Route

The Sentier Cathare is constantly being improved – for example, alternative sections have been added, especially in the central part, offering walkers more options between the eastern and western terminuses. Changes are also sometimes made for other reasons – for example, to take the trail through a village that wants to benefit from passing trade. Furthermore, although the Sentier Cathare mostly follows paths, tracks and roads where the public has a right to walk, some sections are not public, and available only because the landowner has agreed that walkers can go there, but landowners' permissions are withdrawn from time to time, and in such cases the trail has to be diverted. This kind of thing probably happens more frequently than on long-distance routes in Britain, but it usually only affects relatively short sections, and the new route is invariably waymarked quite clearly on the ground.

However, it is important to bear in mind that sections of the Sentier Cathare as shown on French IGN maps may have been modified since those maps appeared. The places where the route, when surveyed for this book, differed from that shown on the then-available 1:25,000 maps, are not always mentioned here. This is because new editions of the maps may soon be published, with the new route shown on them. Furthermore, minor temporary deviations may be

in place where works are being carried out on or close to the trail – for example, tree extraction.

But, once again, none of this need be cause for concern. The Sentier Cathare is well used and well waymarked, and you will be able to follow without any serious difficulty any further modifications that are not described here. When in doubt, simply follow the waymarks on the ground.

Information about recent changes to the route of the trail may be posted in *gîtes d'étape*, tourist information offices and so on.

Castles and Other Features of Interest

As well as Cathar castles, you will find many other places of historical, architectural, archaeological, cultural and environmental interest along the Sentier Cathare, and time set aside for visiting these sites is richly rewarded.

There is an entrance fee for access to most of the Cathar castles, other monuments, museums and so on along the trail. I have included general indications of the times when the castles in particular are open to the public, but these can change from one year to the next, so check the latest information at local tourist information offices (see Appendix 1).

If you plan to visit several castles and other monuments in the area, it is worth buying a *carte inter-sites*, which gives a discounted price for entrance to 16 of these monuments.

Allow time to admire the castles as you encounter them along the trail; this is Quéribus Castle on Stage 4

Bear in mind also that certain castles take quite a while – sometimes a matter of hours – to walk up to and around.

There is only space in this book for brief comments on the Cathar castles and other features of special interest that you will encounter on the Sentier Cathare, but there is plenty more literature describing them, much of it in English. Books, leaflets and other publications are for sale in abundance at many of the castles themselves, and in shops and at information centres round about. Further information about relevant publications, websites and so on can be found in the appendices and elsewhere in this book.

GETTING THERE

The Cathar region can be approached from Britain by plane and/or train in several ways (see the Location Map, pages 8 and 9).

Air

There are major international airports at Toulouse, Montpellier and Barcelona with direct scheduled flights from a number of places in Britain. For example, EasyJet has flights from several British destinations to Barcelona, and from London to Toulouse.

At the time of writing, Ryanair has flights from London to Carcassonne, Montpellier, Nîmes (which is not far from Montpellier) and Perpignan, and from Liverpool to

Nîmes. Ryanair also flies from several British cities to Girona, northeast of Barcelona, and is closer to the Sentier Cathare.

Flybe has flights from Birmingham, Southampton and Bristol to Toulouse and, in the summer, from Birmingham and Southampton to Perpignan.

Relevant information can be obtained from: the French Travel Centre (see Appendix 6); British Airways (within UK – 0870 850 9850, within France – 08 25 82 50 40, www.britishairways.com); Ryanair (within UK – 0871 246 0000, within France – 08 92 55 56 66, www.ryanair.com); Flybe (within UK – 0906 209 0005, outside UK – 00 44 13 922 685 28, www2.flybe.com), and EasyJet (within UK – 0871 244 2366, within France – 08 25 08 25 08, www.easyjet.com).

Rail

The Sentier Cathare begins at Port-la-Nouvelle, at the eastern end of the trail, where there is a railway station with a good local train service between Narbonne to the north (a 20-minute journey to Port-la-Nouvelle) and Perpignan to the south (a 40-minute journey).

There are fast, regular rail connections to Narbonne from Toulouse, Carcassonne, Nîmes and Montpellier.

From Barcelona or Girona you can travel north to Perpignan by rail, and from there on to Port-la-Nouvelle, but there are only a couple

Foix, at the western end of the Sentier Cathare, is an excellent point of arrival or departure for those planning a trek along the trail. It is easily accessible from Toulouse, which has good transport links to Britain.

of fast, direct trains between Barcelona/Girona and Perpignan each day. Otherwise, you have to take slower services and change trains at the frontier.

If you want to start your trek halfway along the Sentier Cathare, at Quillan, head first for Carcassonne, then take the local rail service to Quillan. There is a reasonably regular service along this line, and although trains are sometimes replaced by coaches, they do get you there, and

the journey normally takes less than an hour and a half.

If you want to start at Foix and walk eastwards along the Sentier Cathare, travel first to Toulouse, then take a train south to Foix. The service is pretty good, and the journey takes about an hour and a quarter.

You can of course also travel all the way to Port-la-Nouvelle, Quillan or Foix by train from Britain. Depending on where you start from and which route you decide to take, your journey may involve a number of changes, and it may take more than one day, but it's a lovely way to see the French countryside.

If you travel all the way from Britain by train via Eurostar's Channel Tunnel service, try to change trains in Lille rather than Paris. That way, you only have to cross to another platform, not to the other side of the centre of a city.

Information can be obtained from: the French Travel Centre (see Appendix 6), French Railways (0870 8306030; www.raileurope.co.uk), and Eurostar (08705 186 186; www.eurostar.com).

The website of SNCF, the national French railway service, is at www.sncf.com. It has an English version, and is obviously a good source of information about the times and prices of rail services in France.

The *Thomas Cook European Timetable* for trains across Europe is worth consulting, especially if much of your travelling to and around Sentier Cathare country is by rail. A new edition is published every month, and it is widely available in bookshops in Britain at a cost of around £10.

Road

It is of course also possible to travel to the Cathar region by coach. This is an economical way to travel, but can take a long time (for example, the best part of 24 hours for a journey from London to Perpignan). Information can be obtained from Eurolines (08705 143219; www.nationalex-press.com).

If you travel by road, you can cross France on autoroutes (motorways) all the way, but bear in mind that these are toll roads. They can also be extremely busy in school holiday periods, especially in July and August. In particular, there are often long hold-ups in high summer on the A7 autoroute between Lyon and Orange, which funnels holiday traffic down the Rhône Valley.

There are also useful walkers' links to the Sentier Cathare at Montségur from Lavelanet (on a way-marked local path called Le Chemin Pavé), at Quéribus from Maury (mostly on tracks marked on the IGN 1:25,000 map), and at Stage 4 near the Galamus Gorge from St-Paul-de-Fenouillet (along a country road, the D7). Lavelanat has occasional bus services to Toulouse and Foix. Maury and St-Paul can be reached by bus from Perpignan.

GETTING AROUND

Main roads and railway lines within the Cathar region are shown on the Location Map on pages 8 and 9. There are two main **east–west transport axes**:

- The Narbonne–Carcassonne–Toulouse corridor, through which runs the A61 *autoroute*, and where there are good rail and bus services.

Train services within the Cathar region are not plentiful, but this one is at least very original. It is the summer tourist Train du Pays Cathare et du Fenouillèdes, which runs parallel to the eastern half of the Sentier Cathare, from Rivesaltes to Axat.

- The Perpignan–Quillan–Foix corridor. The main road here is the D117, a single carriageway for most of the way, and running parallel to the Sentier Cathare, often quite close to the trail. There are also bus services , but they are more frequent at the eastern end. For information on bus times, telephone (00 33) (0) 4 68 35 29 02.

A summer tourist train service, the Train du Pays Cathare et du Fenouillèdes, operates between Rivesaltes (north of Perpignan) and Axat (just south of Quillan), via Maury, St-Paul and Caudiès (tel (00 33) (0) 4 68 59 96 18; www.tpcf.fr). Reservations on this service are encouraged.

There are three main **north–south transport axes**:

- The Béziers–Narbonne–Perpignan corridor runs parallel to and close to the Mediterranean coastline. The main road is the A9 *autoroute*, and there are good rail and bus services. Port-la-Nouvelle, at the eastern end of the Sentier Cathare, is in this corridor.
- The Carcassonne–Quillan corridor follows the Aude Valley (Quillan is the halfway point along the Sentier Cathare). The main road here is the D118, a single carriageway for most of the way. There are reasonably good rail and bus services between Carcassonne and Quillan.

The 'Cathar knights' – huge modern sculptures by Jacques Tissinier that overlook the A61 motorway near Narbonne; the knights greet many visitors who travel from the north to the Cathar region

- The Toulouse–Foix–Ax-les-Thermes corridor follows the Ariège Valley (Foix is at the western end of the Sentier Cathare), and here the main road is the N20, which is partly double carriageway and partly single. There are good rail and bus services along the corridor.

Elsewhere in Cathar castle **country rail services** are non-existent and **bus services** scarce. Buses do serve several towns and villages away from the main transport corridors, but these are often mainly for taking children to and from school, so may be infrequent, and not run at all during school holidays.

Most of the information offices listed in Appendix 1 should be able to give you telephone numbers for bus companies, and for **taxi services** that operate within the region, some of which also offer **baggage-carrying services**. A few contact numbers for taxi and baggage-carrying services, supplied by the tourist office in Quillan, can be found in Appendix 2.

The roads of intermediate and minor status that wind across the hills and valleys of the countryside within the main transport corridors often carry relatively little traffic. They can be quite pleasant to drive or cycle along if you are not in a hurry, but you do have to be constantly alert for vehicles that may suddenly come hurtling towards you around the bend just ahead. Nor should you be surprised if someone suddenly appears out of nowhere behind you, and attempts to overtake at the slightest opportunity.

Please also note that such roads often change their number when they cross departmental boundaries. Thus, for example, the road going north from St-Paul-de-Fenouillet towards the Galamus Gorge is the D7 – there, it is in the Pyrénées-Orientales department. Halfway through the gorge, the road passes into the Aude department and becomes the D10.

Finally, if your prefer travels with a **donkey**, ask tourist offices for addresses of places that hire these splendid beasts for treks in the region. One such enterprise is based in Cailla, on Stage 6 of the Main Route of the trail: **Zig'ânes, 4 Rue des Lavoirs, 11140 Cailla (tel** (00 33) (0) 4 68 20 57 73, info@ziganes.com, www.ziganes.com).

ACCOMMODATION

Detailed information about accommodation along the Sentier Cathare can be found in Appendix 1. The following section describes accommodation in the region more generally.

Accommodation in Cathar castle country is plentiful, wide-ranging, and generally of high quality, extending from simple campsites to luxury hotels. Good starting points for making enquiries and gathering relevant literature are the French Travel Centre in London (see Appendix 2) or a tourist information office in the Cathar region (see Appendix 1). Many bookshops in Britain sell guides to accommodation in France, with listings of hotels in particular.

Most hotels, *gîtes*, campsites, etc., are open from Easter to October, and many, especially those in or near cities and large towns, are open all or most of the year.

This is a popular area with tourists, so it is highly recommended that you check in advance room/bed availability, and reserve accommodation before you arrive. This is especially true for July and August, when many establishments will be fully booked.

If you have access to the Internet, you will find that many establishments, in all price ranges, not only have e-mail addresses, but also websites that give you information about their facilities, and which often invite you to book accommodation online.

Many proprietors along the trail can understand at least some English, but for the purpose of booking accommodation – as for communicating generally while in the region – it is a good idea to have a few survival words and phrases in French at your disposal.

There are several **campsites** along the Sentier Cathare, and Appendix 1 lists some of the principal managed ones. For information about such campsites throughout France, see www.campingfrance.com. Several other smaller and more informal campsites can also be found along the trail, especially in the summer months – for example, on land adjacent to some *gîtes d'étape* or on nearby private farmland. The tourist information offices and *mairies* listed in Appendix 1 may be able to give information about these.

Gîtes d'étape are rather like youth hostels. They are reasonably priced and most towns and sizeable villages have at least one. Many are run as private enterprises, but often they are managed by the local *commune*. Like youth hostels, they generally offer excellent value for money, although they vary a good deal in size, comfort and facilities. You can

generally count on getting meals there, but if not there is usually a café, restaurant or grocer's nearby. On *gîtes d'étape* generally, see www.gite-etape.com.

The Sentier Cathare and other long-distance paths in France are generally planned so that there are *gîtes d'étape* at the end of every stage. The website www.gites-refuges.com, which is in English as well as French, is a useful source of information about *gîtes* and other types of simple accommodation along the Sentier Cathare and in the wider Cathar region.

Gîtes rurals are self-catering houses, cottages or apartments in the countryside or along the coast. These too vary considerably in size and facilities, but their quality is generally good. The organisation to contact is Gîtes de France, at La Maison des Gîtes de France et du Tourisme Vert, 59 Rue Saint-Lazare, 75439 Paris Cedex 09, tel (00 33) (0)1 49 70 75 75, www.gites-de-france.fr.

There are a large number of **chambres d'hôtes** in Cathar castle country. These are the French equivalent of bed and breakfast, and these days more and more are advertising

Hotels and bed and breakfasts are dotted along the Sentier Cathare, but for those seeking simpler, inexpensive accommodation, gîtes d'étape (like this one signposted on Stage 5 of the trail's North Variant) are plentiful

themselves as 'bed and breakfast'. They offer excellent value for money and are generally of a very high quality. Gîtes de France also promotes *chambres d'hôtes*, and is a good source of information about them. *Bed & Breakfast in France 2004* (about £13), a co-publication by the AA and the French Gîtes de France, lists over 3000 bed and breakfasts around France.

Hotels are not quite so abundant, but they can be found in towns like Foix and Quillan, and in large villages like Montségur and Cucugnan that are close to the best-known Cathar castles.

Hotels which bear the Logis de France label seem to be invariably reliable and good value, and the Logis de France guidebook to hotels that have been awarded its label is sold in some bookshops in Britain and France. Their central reservations telephone number is (00 33) (0)1 45 84 83 84 and their website is at www.logis-de-fr.fr. The famous Michelin Red Guide to hotels in France can also be invaluable. Lists of hotels in and near particular towns can be looked up on www.viamichelin.com.

Auberge is a term adopted by a wide variety of establishments. Some are *gîtes d'étape*, others are hotels, but what they generally have in common is a restaurant of some sort on the premises.

The route of the Sentier Cathare is described in this book in an east–west direction, and divided into 12 day-stages. The Route Summary Table on page 37 gives distance, estimated walking time, ascent, etc.

The section for each stage of the trail gives the following:

- A **brief summary of the stage**, with particular reference to Cathar castles along the way, the landscape, and the severity of the stage if it is more than average.
- **Key information** about the stage: distance, estimated walking time, altitude, total ascent and descent, 1:25,000 maps, and **navigation** along the trail.
- A **description of the stage**, from east to west. This description consists mostly of directions for following the trail, with principal points of interest (Cathar castles, other monuments, and so forth) highlighted.
- Notes for **west–east** walkers, especially on particular path junctions and other features to look out for, so as to be sure of staying on the route.
- Notes on **points of interest** along the stage that are highlighted in the route description, especially Cathar castles.
- A **sketch map** of the stage. Numbers in brackets in the text refer to numbered points on the corresponding sketch map(s).

Please note that to minimise any doubt about the direction you should be taking, guidance is occasionally in the form of 'take the path going west', 'head east from this junction', and so on. To be able to make best use of these directions, you are advised to carry a compass, and be able to use it when necessary.

PLANNING A TREK ALONG THE CATHAR WAY

In this guide the route of the Sentier Cathare is divided into 12 stages which, in theory, can be walked in a day (see Map of Stages, pages 10 and 11). Stage 1, starting at Port-la-Nouvelle, is at the eastern end of the trail; Stage 12, ending in Foix, is at the western end. There are facilities for overnight accommodation at both ends of each stage, usually including (and sometimes consisting only of) a *gîte d'étape*.

However, some stages are quite long and tough, and/or have interesting castles and other features worth exploring en route, so ways to vary the route to suit your interests and abilities are described in the following sections. This information may seem confusing if you haven't already studied the details of the trail, so you may want to skim through the route descriptions, and study the Location Map (pages 8 and 9) and the 1:25,000 maps, to see where the various alternatives routes actually go, before returning to this section.

Alternative Routes

As mentioned earlier, there are various alternative routes on the central stages of the trail, and no one principal path from Port-la-Nouvelle to Foix has been officially designated. However, it seems helpful to suggest to readers a route that might be best regarded as the principal one from one end to the other. That route is referred to here as the **Main Route,** and a second option is described as the **North Variant**. This branches off the Main Route about halfway along Stage 4 and rejoins it about halfway along Stage 7 (see map, pages 10 and 11.)

The main advantage of the Main Route over the North Variant is that the former links all nine Cathar castles referred to earlier. The North Variant does not pass by the Cathar castles of Fenouillet (Stage 5) and Puilaurens (Stage 6).

However, the Main Route does not pass through the astonishing **Galamus Gorge** (Stage 4), nor through **Quillan**, a town about halfway between Port-la-Nouvelle and Foix, whereas the North Variant does.

There are public transport links to Quillan from Carcassonne and Toulouse, so it is a good place to start or begin a trek if you want to walk only half or less of the trail's full distance. The town also has shops, banks and plentiful overnight accommodation. By contrast, the Main Route, after running through Axat on

The trail is conventionally divided into 12 stages, but if you want to walk at a leisurely pace and break up some of the longer stages, this can easily be done – Cucugnan, for example, on Stage 4, offers plenty of accommodation

Stage 6, traverses remote country, which is certainly delightful, but where overnight accommodation is limited and shops and buses almost non-existent.

The main body of this book consists of a section on each stage of the trail, both along the Main Route and the North Variant, and there is also a section describing the waymarked link between Stage 5 of the North Variant and Stage 5 of the Main Route. Following this link allows you to walk through the Galamus Gorge, and you also see all nine Cathar castles. However, it makes for a very long and tiring Stage 5, especially as it is recommended that you leave the trail for an hour or two to visit the Fenouillet castles, and you may also need to walk another kilometre or so at the end to reach accommodation at a place called Lapradelle. So if you use the link, it would be best to take two days to walk Stage 5, breaking at Caudiès-de-Fenouillèdes.

If you want to see all nine Cathar castles and pass through Quillan, you could keep to the Main Route as far as Axat, then take a bus or taxi to Quillan. An afternoon and an evening bus are currently timetabled to run most days between Axat and Quillan. The service operator is GEP Vidal (tel (00 33) (0) 4 68 61 30 30). For information about taxi services, see Appendix 2, or telephone the tourist office in Quillan or the Maison des Pyrénées du Pays Cathare near Axat (see Appendix 1). From Quillan, follow Stage 7 of the North Variant to Coudons, and pick up the Main Route again there.

Some walkers may want to cut out the first two long stages of the trail, and start with the third stage at Tuchan, near Aguilar Castle, the easternmost of the Cathar fortresses. To reach Tuchan you could take a bus from Perpignan 's central bus station (*gare routière*) to Estagel (there is a reasonably frequent service), then a taxi to Tuchan (tel (00 33) (0) 4 68 29 then 00 34 or 00 00 or 08 55).

Some other relatively minor alternative sections are also included in the route description. Stage 6 of the Main Route gives options for two end points – Quirbajou and Labeau – both of which have a *gîte d'étape*. Likewise, Stage 8 gives options for two end points – Espezel and Belvis – thus offering a wider choice of accommodation.

Places of Interest

There are several villages and other places off the Sentier Cathare that are worth visiting in their own right, if you have the time, and/or that offer facilities not necessarily found along the trail itself. Some of these are mentioned in the route description, e.g. St-Paul-de-Fenouillet is a town a couple of kilometres south of Stage 4 that has shops, hotels, bus services, buildings of archaeological interest, and so on. Ways of reaching that town on foot from the trail are summarised in Stage 4 of the Main Route description.

ROUTE SUMMARY

For each stage of the trail, the estimated **distance**, **walking time**, **altitude**, total approximate **ascent** and total approximate **descent** (for east–west walkers) are summarised in the Route Summary Table on page 37. These are based on the 'official' estimates published in France. The **1:25,000 maps** needed for each stage are also listed in the Summary Table. (If the estimated time for any stage is likely to be significantly different for

ROUTE SUMMARY TABLE, EAST–WEST

Name	Start Point	Finish Point	Distance (km)	Time	High Point (m)	Total Ascent (m)	Total Descent (m)	1:25,000 Map(s)
Stage 1	Port-la-Nouvelle	Durban-Corbières	29.0	6h45	300	600	510	2547OT
Stage 2	Durban-Corbières	Tuchan	28.0	7h00	350	800	730	2547OT; 2447OT
Stage 3	Tuchan	Duilhac-s-Peyrepertuse	23.5	6h30	600	750	560	2447OT
Stage 4 Main Route	Duilhac-s-Peyrepertuse	Prugnanes	17.5	4h30	670	650	670	2447OT
Stage 4 North Variant	*Duilhac-s-Peyrepertuse*	*Camps-sur-l'Agly*	*19.0*	*5h00*	*670*	*560*	*400*	*2447OT*
Stage 5 Main Route	Prugnanes	Puilaurens village	18.5	4h45	690	450	330	2348ET
Stage 5 North Variant	*Camps-sur-l'Agly*	*Bugarach*	*12.0*	*3h45*	*910*	*500*	*560*	*2347OT*
Stage 6 Main Route	Puilaurens village	Quirbajou	23.5	6h00	810	670	320	2348ET; 2248ET
Stage 6 North Variant	*Bugarach*	*Quillan*	*23.5*	*6h15*	*825*	*700*	*880*	*2347OT*
Stage 7 Main Route	Quirbajou	Puivert	22.5	5h45	1150	480	810	2347OT; 2227OT
Stage 7 North Variant	*Quillan*	*Puivert*	*20.5*	*5h45*	*850*	*700*	*500*	*2347OT; 2247OT*
Stage 8	Puivert	Espezel	17.0	4h30	930	600	190	2227OT
Stage 9	Espezel	Comus	20.0	5h15	1350	500	230	2247OT; 2148ET
Stage 10	Comus	Montségur	14.5	3h30	1170	500	750	2148ET; 2247OT
Stage 11	Montségur	Roquefixade	17.0	4h15	1025	550	710	2247OT; 2147ET
Stage 12	Roquefixade	Foix	18.0	5h00	930	500	890	2147ET
Totals via Main Route	**Port-la-Nouvelle**	**Foix**	**249.0**	**63h45**	**1350**	**7050**	**6700**	
Totals via North Variant	**Port-la-Nouvelle**	**Foix**	**242.0**	**63h45**	**1350**	**7260**	**6910**	

This table does not give the distances, times, etc., for the link between Stage 5 (North Variant) and Stage 5 (Main Route), nor for routes that use the alternative end points of Labeau (on Stage 6, Main Route) and Belvis (on Stage 8). See the relevant route description sections for further details.

'Time' is estimated walking time – see the notes on this in the 'Route Summary' section.

Key to Maps:

2547OT	(Durban-Corbières/Leucate)	2248ET	(Axat/Quérigut/Gorges de l'Aude)
2447OT	(Tuchan)	2247OT	(Lavelanet)
2348ET	(Pradés/St-Paul-de-Fenouillet)	2148ET	(Ax-les-Thermes)
2347OT	(Quillan)	2147ET	(Foix/Tarascon-sur-Ariège)

west–east walkers, this is noted, and of course total *ascent* for east–west walkers will be total *descent* for west–east walkers, and vice versa.)

A few caveats need to be made about the estimated walking times given in the Summary Table. The first is that the times seem to have been estimated by some pretty fit French hikers! Other walkers may find that these estimates make for a demanding timetable, especially in the easternmost stages, and especially if a heavy pack is being carried. It might be wise, assuming that you are a walker of average ability, to add, say, 10 minutes for every hour of the 'official' time – at least at first, until a pattern emerges and you can make any necessary adjustments yourself to the estimated times.

The estimated walking times do not make allowances for any significant pauses or diversions. In particular, you will need to allow a good deal of extra time to visit the Cathar castles that lie close to the trail. Advice for the time to allow in each case is given in the relevant section.

All things considered, if you are planning to walk the whole route, and want to do so at a reasonably comfortable pace with time to visit the main monuments, it would be wise to allow at least 14 days for the whole trek. There are several places with accommodation en route where the longer stages, which are mostly at the eastern end, might be broken. For example, Roquefort-sur-Corbières is a

good point at which to break Stage 1, and Stage 3 could comfortably be broken at Cucugnan.

STOCKING UP

There are many towns and large villages on or close to the Sentier Cathare where you can count on finding at least one store, such as a **supermarket** or *épicerie* (grocer's-cum-general store), which is open on most days throughout the year. But bear in mind that, like almost everything else in France, apart from restaurants, they will probably be closed for two or three hours from midday. Most such places also have a **chemist** (*pharmacie* – look out for a flashing green cross), **baker** (*boulangerie*) and other shops.

Banks and **post offices** are more widely spaced out. If you can't find a post office and you only want a few stamps, try a **tobacconist** – they usually sell them.

However, some villages are now without permanent shops, or they have such facilities, but they only open at peak holiday periods, when there are more people around. '**Travelling shops**' – vans and lorries loaded up with food and everyday items – usually visit these villages, acting as mobile *épiceries*. Sometimes the postman, arriving in a yellow van at great speed, drops off bread and newspapers to a remote village or hamlet. Appendix 1 indicates which villages along the trail may not have permanent shops, but there is a town

Some villages along the trail (such as this one, Duilhac-sous-Peyrepertuse, Stage 3) are keen to advertise their shops and services

or village where you can stock up, on or close to almost every stage of the Sentier Cathare. In addition, *gîtes* and farms along the way will often offer for sale to passersby cheese, milk, honey, fruit, bread and other essential supplies.

Some of the simpler accommodation establishments will not accept payment by credit card, and this can also be the case in small shops, bars and restaurants. They will only accept payment by French cheque or cash, so carry a good stock of euros in your rucksack!

MAPS

The sketch maps in this book offer only an indication of the key features along the trail, and it is strongly rec-

ommended that those who tackle the Sentier Cathare (or who walk anywhere in the Cathar region) also equip themselves with the relevant 1:25,000 maps published by the Institut Géographique National (IGN). These excellent maps contain very detailed topographical information.

The Sentier Cathare is shown on these map, and although the route has been altered in a few places since the maps were published, overall this concerns only a relatively small proportion of the whole, and diversions are always clearly waymarked on the ground.

The **1:25,000** maps needed for each stage of the Sentier Cathare and its various alternative sections are given in the Route Summary Table on page 37, and in the individual route description sections. There are eight in total and they are as follows:

2547OT (Durban-Corbières/Leucate)
2447OT (Tuchan)
2348ET (Prades/St-Paul-de-Fenouillet)
2347OT (Quillan)
2248ET (Axat/Quérigut/Gorges de l'Aude)
2247OT (Lavelanet)
2148ET (Ax-les-Thermes)
2147ET (Foix/Tarascon-sur-Ariège).

The French 1:25,000 maps are invaluable – and fit neatly into a rucksack pocket

All the 1:25,000 maps that cover the route of the Sentier Cathare show long-distance paths, local walking routes and a lot of other information of value to tourists, and all are into at least their second edition. You can tell which edition a particular copy of a map is by looking at the number in brackets in the title of map on the spine of the map cover. For example, the second edition of the Quillan map (dated 2000) has on the cover spine '2347 OT Quillan (2)'. If you buy maps in shops in France, check that you get the latest edition – copies of older editions may still be mixed up with copies of newer editions on the shops' shelves. The newer editions of all 1:25,000 maps are being marketed as *Cartes de Randonnée* (walkers' maps).

A grid of numbered kilometre squares covers the 1:25,000 maps for the Sentier Cathare, and they can be used with global positioning devices (a GPS symbol is shown on the front of these maps).

Many newsagent's, bookshops and supermarkets in France sell IGN maps, but prices vary from shop to shop. A 1:25,000 map costs around 10 Euros (about £7).

The publisher **Rando éditions** has produced a series of **1:50,000** maps covering the French Pyrenees and their northern foothills. They are also called *Cartes de randonnées*, and they use IGN cartography. In this series, Number 9, Montségur, covers an area between Quillan and Foix,

and thus includes the western half of the Sentier Cathare. Its price is around 10 Euros.

For **route planning** purposes, IGN's series of **1:100,000** maps (the **Cartes topographiques Top 100** series, or **Cartes de promenade**) is very helpful. Numbers 71 (St-Gaudens/Andorre) and 72 (Béziers Perpignan) cover most of Cathar castle country, including the whole route of the Sentier Cathare.

IGN's **1:250,000** maps (their **Cartes régionales** series) are designed for route planning by road. Cathar castle country is covered by Midi-Pyrénées (R16) and Languedoc-Roussillon (R17).

In France, the 1:100,000 and 1:250,000 maps currently cost around 5 Euros each.

IGN's website is at www.ign.fr, and is in French only. Their maps and other products can be bought via that website, but with postage to Britain and the cost of currency transfer, the final prices seem to be a little higher than those charged by British suppliers of the same maps. British suppliers include:

Stanfords, 12–14 Long Acre, Covent Garden, London WC2E 9LP, tel 020 7836 1321, sales@stanfords.co.uk, www.stanfords.co.uk.

The Map Shop, 15 High Street, Upton-upon-Severn, Worcs WR8 0HJ, tel 01684 593146 (Freephone 0800 085 4080), themapshop@btinternet.com, www.themapshop.co.uk.

WEATHER

Recorded messages in French giving the weather forecast for the *département* that you are in can be obtained by dialling 08 92 68 02 + the number of the *département* (Aude – 11, Pyrénées-Orientales – 66, Ariège – 09).

In general, the weather in the Cathar region is very agreeable. Nevertheless, although the Mediterranean is never very far away, it would be a mistake to imagine that this region is similar to torrid Andalusia or bone-dry Crete. Rather, the weather is like that of Kent – only more so. Winter days are often cold and blustery, but springtime usually starts earlier, the summers are hotter and last longer, and there are more sunny days throughout the year.

However, the climate here has a great capacity to surprise. For example, a hot day in summer can start sunny and clear, but a tremendous thunderstorm may suddenly build up in the early afternoon. Typically, that storm could vent its fury in less than half an hour (but not always). In winter there might be weeks of mild, dry weather, followed by a day in which half a metre or more of snow is suddenly dumped on higher ground.

A feature of this region that may also surprise is the occasional fierce and unrelenting winds, one of which is the **tramontane**, which comes from the northwest. Its often cold temperature can be guarded against with adequate warm clothing and, insofar as it may blow away the clouds and let the sun shine through, it can be welcome. But take great care if you are walking on a hill or mountain ridge when the *tramontane* is at full blast.

You will often see, incidentally, lines of wind turbines stretched out across high plateaux. These are, in fact, now almost as characteristic of Cathar castle country as the castles themselves. But on the Sentier Cathare at present, you pass very close to such turbines only on Stage 1.

The climate can vary a great deal from east to west in the region. On any given day, the weather in the east, near the Mediterranean coast, may be hot and dry, while in the west conditions could be more Atlantic – cooler, with cloud cover and showers. The vegetation shows corresponding differences. For example, the easternmost stage of the Sentier Cathare crosses dry, open plateaux covered in *garrigue* vegetation – scented, often-spiky Mediterranean shrubs and herbs. By contrast, the westernmost stage of the trail winds through humid deciduous forest, where beech trees grow to regal proportions.

Note in particular that the first two stages of the trail (from Port-la-Nouvelle to Tuchan), although impressive in many respects, are also particularly long, dry and exposed, and the weather here can be especially hot at any time from early June to mid-September. Also, you don't encounter a Cathar castle until almost the end of the second stage. Advice is given under Planning a Trek, above, on how to travel direct to Tuchan to start your walk there, if you want to cut out the first two stages.

EQUIPMENT AND WATER

The climate changes with altitude. Near sea level you will find that light clothing and trainers are perfectly adequate, even on some winter days, but on the hills and mountains you should wear walking boots and carry adequate warm and waterproof clothing at all times of the year.

On the assumption that you are planning to walk the Sentier Cathare between Easter and early autumn, you should bring the same range of clothing and equipment that you would pack for, say, a summer walking tour of any upland range in England. Make sure that includes light clothing (such as T-shirts and shorts), because, if you are lucky with

Carry plenty of drinking water, and look out for signs like this one (Les Bordes, Stage 5, Main Route), which indicate sources of water that are safe to drink

the weather, you may find that you wear little else.

If you already have some experience of walking in various types of terrain in Britain, you won't need to be told that you should always carry equipment like a good **map** and a **compass**, especially if you are going into the hills. If you have not done any great amount of walking before coming to Cathar castle country, the best advice is to read up about it beforehand, for instance by getting hold of a copy of *The Hillwalker's Manual* by Bill Birkett (Cicerone).

Two things, however, do need to be stressed. The first is that you need to carry a lot of **water** when walking the Sentier Cathare, or anywhere in the region. On a day's walk here, you will almost certainly build up much, much more of a thirst than you would when walking in Britain. This is especially true of hot, summer days, but the extent to which that advice applies in cooler periods is surprising. Some of the villages and hamlets along the trail have welcome water fountains and taps that dispense drinking water (*eau potable*), but unfortunately you can't rely on finding sources of drinking water in all such settlements. In any case, it is advisable to drink only from fountains and taps that have an *eau potable* sign next to them.

The second point is that you need to carry and apply to your person a liberal quantity of effective **sun screen**. In this respect, the region

43

Drinking-water fountain in the centre of Prugnanes (beginning of Stage 5, Main Route)

the following needs to be borne in mind.

The **sudden storms** mentioned above can cause rivers to rise with amazing rapidity – dry streambeds can become raging torrents within a matter of hours.

Heavy storms may carve deep gullies in paths and tracks, making them difficult to walk along. Generally, such *passages ravinés* along the trail are repaired quickly, but you will probably come across at least one or two such sections if you walk the whole length of the Sentier Cathare.

The storms may of course be accompanied by **lightning**. If you can shelter in a refuge while a storm rages, well and good, but the likelihood is that the storm will break before you can reach one. In that case, the best thing to do is to sit on your rucksack in open ground after laying aside anything metal, like walking sticks. You will get very wet, of course, but you will minimise the risk of being struck by lightning, and in such weather conditions you stand a good chance of drying out quickly in the sun once the storm has passed.

Lightning may also cause **fire**, as can other things, not least the negligence of people who toss cigarette stubs out of cars and trains.

does bear comparison with Andalusia and Crete.

You will also need, of course, equipment for overnight stops. How much you take will obviously depend on whether you are backpacking or staying in *gîtes* or other accommodation, but given that the weather here is often hot and dry, there's a lot to be said for travelling as light as possible while on trek.

RISKS

A few other warnings are called for, but don't let these deter you from walking the Sentier Cathare or visiting Cathar castle country – it is on the whole a pretty safe place. However,

*'Boar shooting in progress. Take care' –
but the translation is probably superfluous*

Fortunately, this part of France suffers much less from fires in forest and undergrowth than does hotter, drier Provence, further east. But, if you ever find yourself anywhere near an uncontrolled fire, move away from it as quickly as possible. Flames can move across the ground with startling speed, especially when a strong wind is blowing. Needless to say, walkers should take great care not to start a fire themselves.

If you are walking anywhere in this region from September to February, you should not be surprised to hear occasionally the sharp crack of **gunfire**. The guns are probably being fired by hunters tracking down **wild boar** or, on the higher ground, **deer**. During this period in particular you may also see signs hung alongside footpaths warning you that shooting is taking place in the area, although it really is very unlikely that you will be shot. Hunters have to comply with strict safety regulations, including not firing across footpaths. Just stick carefully to the waymarked path.

You have even less cause for concern if you ever actually see a wild boar – the sight of anything resembling *homo sapiens* will cause it to turn on its heels and dash off without a second's hesitation. **Wolves** and **bears** also live in Cathar castle country, but in extremely small numbers. It

is true that they eat sheep and other livestock for breakfast, but your chances of meeting one of these creatures is almost infinitely small.

Pyrenean sheep dogs – big, beautiful, white-haired creatures – are often employed by farmers to guard flocks of **sheep** and **goats** while they graze. These dogs are usually unaccompanied by shepherds, and if you pass one of them, they may utter a few warning barks in your direction, but they present no danger to walkers – unless you are accompanied by a dog. In these, as in all circumstances, keep it well under control. Pyrenean sheep dogs are trained to issue summary justice to bears, wolves and

45

These are not real bears, but there really are bears in these parts; opposite is the Maison des Pyrénées du Pays Cathare, an information centre near Axat, Stage 6 (Main Route)

stray dogs that threaten their flock, so don't give them reason to take issue with your domestic pet.

Sheep and cattle are often fenced in, and even high up on open country you will come across wire fences. They rarely present an insuperable barrier, but always be careful how you cross them – they might be electrified (some electric fences are powered by solar panels).

Snakes are rarely sighted, and the majority of those that live here are not poisonous, but you should obviously give a wide berth to any that you may encounter.

However, there is a quite different species which can take on a snake-like appearance, and which is perhaps the most dangerous creature that you are likely to encounter. It is in fact a caterpillar. In the early spring, especially beneath or near pine trees, you may see curious, worm-like lines of hairy brown caterpillars winding across the ground – these are **processional caterpillars**, whose winter residence is a cottonwool cocoon high up

46

in a pine tree. They chomp on the pine needles and can leave whole forests devastated. In spring they come down to earth, form head-to-tail chains, and wander around looking for somewhere to bury themselves. Don't touch them or even get too close to them – they have a nasty sting, and above all, if you have a dog with you, keep it well away from the caterpillars, or you could be facing a distressing trip to the nearest vet.

When you arrive in Cathar castle country, take a note of telephone numbers to ring in case of **emergency**. Those numbers are posted up in information offices, *gîtes*, hotels and so on. But if you ever need to telephone for help, or to report an accident or a fire, and you are not sure who best to call, the number to ring is 18. This is for the French fire service, the **Sapeurs Pompiers**, and it deals with many types of emergency. But bear in mind that **mobile telephones will not always work in remoter areas of countryside**, and always ensure that you have adequate insurance, in case you need to be rescued, or need emergency medical treatment.

On Stage 6 of the Cathar Way, below Puilaurens Castle, one of the best-preserved of the fortresses associated with the Cathars

STAGE 1
Port-la-Nouvelle to Durban-Corbières

This is one of the longest and hardest of all 12 stages of the Sentier Cathare. You cross no fewer than four ranges of limestone hills – dry plateaux with no water or shade. Start early, and be prepared for a long, thirsty and possibly windy day, although the rewards include glorious views over the Mediterranean coastline and the rolling Corbières hills.

For much of this section you walk alongside a very diverse, sweet-scented, but often impenetrable form of Mediterranean vegetation known as the *garrigue*. You also pass through and alongside many vineyards, from where the richly flavoured and much-exported Corbières wine is produced.

Distance	29km
Walking time	6 hours 45 min
Altitude	From 5m above sea level to 300m
Ascent/Descent	600m/510m
IGN 1:25,000 Map	2547OT (Durban-Corbières Leucate); Port-la-Nouvelle is in map fold 10A, Durban-Corbières is in map fold 3A

Navigation
There is very little waymarking through Port-la-Nouvelle. The official route takes you past the town hall and a supermarket, but if you want to leave the town by a shorter route, follow the **Alternative** described below.

In the summer of 2005, fire destroyed much vegetation on and around the Garrigue Haute, the limestone plateau between Port-la-Nouvelle and Roquefort-des-Corbières. The burnt-out landscape will take some time to recover.

The Plat des Courbines (between **(10)** and **(12)** on the map) is a huge, uninhabited *garrigue*-covered plateau. There are few clear landmarks, so pay particular attention to checking off the Sentier Cathare waymarks as you pass them – especially in misty conditions. This advice applies to all the other limestone plateaux that you cross on this and other stages of the walk, but Courbines is the most challenging.

From outside the railway station of **Port-la-Nouvelle (1)**, go down the Avenue Jean Moulin, in the direction of the coast. Turn right where it meets the Boulevard de l'Avenir. When you come to a roundabout, turn right into the Boulevard Francis Vals. A supermarket (Super U) is on the left. Pass a sports complex on the right, then turn right at the next roundabout. This road, heading west, leaves the town, crosses the railway line, then comes down to the north–south D709 **(2)**, where there is a Sentier Cathare signpost.

Alternative A shorter but less attractive route out of the town is as follows. With the station behind you, turn right down Rue Guy Moquet. Walk parallel to the railway

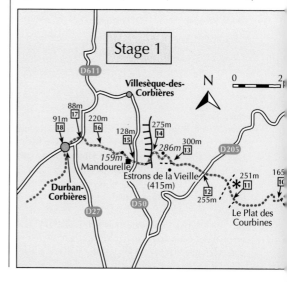

line, and just before reaching a road bridge, bear left, then turn right along a road that goes over the railway line. You come down to the D709 at point **(2)**.

The beach at Port-la-Nouvelle, at the far eastern end of the Sentier Cathare

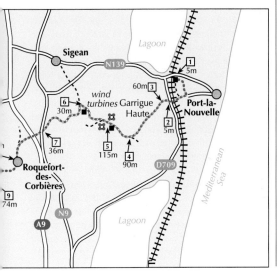

Cross the D709 and climb the rough-surfaced road rising into the hills directly ahead. When the route, now a gravel track, forks three ways (3), take the track on the far left, then fork right a little way ahead. You now cross a large, open limestone plateau – the appropriately named Garrigue Haute.

Follow a stony track, running roughly parallel to a power line on the left. The track eventually bends to the right and you can see wind turbines on the highest ground to the right.

The track descends into a valley on the left, where it is joined by another track with yellow signs indicating the routes of local walks (4). The track climbs gently towards the wind turbines. On the left is an avenue of cypress trees leading to an old stone building, now in ruins.

Go straight ahead at a crossing of tracks by the **wind turbines (5)** and start to descend. After a short distance, take a right fork. The track bends to the right and passes under a power line. A smaller, rougher track goes off to the left. Take that. It descends fairly steeply and soon joins a larger track coming from the right. On your left you pass another substantial stone building in ruins. The track winds downhill again, emerging into an open area and crossing a stream.

Now turn sharp left (6) at a junction with a route that connects the town of Sigean to the Sentier Cathare. There follows a long, winding section on a track that mainly runs close to a stream on the left, with vineyards on the right. At one point you pass through part of a pine forest, and a little later the path heads straight up a small embankment to cross an area of *garrigue*.

You reach another vineyard and follow its left-hand edge, with an embankment on the left. Descend to a semi-open area and go straight across. The track on the other side takes you across a stream on the left, via a substantial concrete bridge. The track bends to the right to go through a narrow tunnel under the N9 (7). You are now on a minor road which in turn goes under the A9 motorway.

The town of **Roquefort-des-Corbières (8)** now comes into view. Turn left at a road junction and shortly afterwards enter Roquefort. At a T-junction, turn right. At the far end of this road, turn left and go up the Rue des Trois Moulins. At the top of the road, bear right.

Near the edge of the town, take a right fork along a road that is signposted after a short while as the Chemin de la Trillole. The ground rises a little and you reach the edge of open country, with vineyards covering most of the land ahead. Keep on the principal lane, ignoring another one forking off to the right, but after a few hundred metres, be careful to take a right fork where the lane divides **(9)**.

Once you eventually reach the end of the vineyards, the track starts to climb into the hills straight ahead, reaching a col in open country **(10)**. ▶

Go straight on, and shortly follow the main track as it swerves right and starts to go downhill. The track reaches the bottom of a steep-sided valley, swings sharp left and soon starts to make a long, sinuous climb up to the dry limestone plateau ahead.

Sun-baked Roquefort-des-Corbières

From here there is a superb view back towards the coast, and of the adjacent inland lagoons and Roquefort-des-Corbières.

You now cross the expansive Plat des Courbines. In about the centre of the plateau, the track reaches a fork where the trail turns right **(11)**. Not long after that, it forks left. Some time later, the track finally starts to wind downhill – on the right are two water-filled wells built of dry stone. The track reaches a T-junction of tracks where you go straight on, following a small path into the conifer plantation ahead. After winding about over stony ground, this path eventually comes out onto the D205 **(12)**.

Cross the road and climb the track directly opposite. On reaching the top of the rise, emerge onto another limestone plateau and go under a large power line. The track terraces along the side of a hill called the Estrons de la Vieille. When you come to a significant fork in the track **(13)**, turn right and start to go downhill more steeply.

Towards the bottom of this hill the route takes a number of complicated twists and turns, so follow the waymarking carefully. Fork left, then almost immediately turn left off the track onto a footpath that winds through the undergrowth and meets another track. Turn left again – on the right is a small hill at 286m with a pylon on top. On reaching the corner of a cultivated field, turn right and pass, on your right, a ruined stone building. The track bears to the left around the edge of the cultivated patch, climbs a little and reaches a point where it bears left. At that point, take a path going off to the right, and very soon reach the top of some impressive limestone cliffs **(14)**, looking down into the valley below.

The stony path twists down the cliff to reach a semi-open area that may be a former pasture, now becoming overgrown. Here, the Sentier Cathare climbs a little to the left, then descends and becomes a rocky track that traverses the side of a hill spur to the left. At the bottom of the slope, pass around the edge of a rough pasture on the right, then emerge onto the D50 opposite a barn with a red roof **(15)**.

Cross that road and follow the track directly ahead – a fine stone farmhouse called Mandourelle is just above, on the left. The track follows the right-hand edge of a field in a wide valley bottom. Follow the track as it bends to the right and starts to climb the side of a small tributary valley.

Near the top of the small valley, the track bends to the left, passes to the right of a small, conifer-planted hill at 159m, then descends to the floor of a valley at the corner of a vineyard. Go up the track straight ahead. It bends to the right and climbs steadily, now with dense Mediterranean vegetation on both sides.

The track suddenly ends and the route becomes a path which at first scrambles up a steep embankment (this may be quite slippery in wet conditions). The path then winds up to the top of the hill from where **(16)** you finally look down on this stage's goal, the village of Durban-Corbières.

The path winds downhill to the left, then meets a wide track, which you follow. After passing a smallholding on the right, the track becomes a surfaced lane and descends abruptly to meet the D611 **(17)**. Turn left, then immediately right over a road bridge that crosses a wide river.

Continue alongside the main road into **Durban-Corbières (18)**.

Notes for west–east walkers
Between (15) and (14). After crossing almost bare rock, you pass along the right-hand edge of what looks like an overgrown former pasture. Descend a little and come to a corner of that overgrown area. Here the waymarking may be a little confusing – you **must turn right here**, towards the cliffs on the right.

Between (14) and (13). Be careful to follow the waymarked route through all the twists and turns here. In particular, with the pylon on a small hill at 286m on the left, be sure to find, and turn right onto, a small path going off the track into the undergrowth. The path meets another track, where you turn right, then climb to the track junction at point **(13)**.

Be careful in passing through Roquefort-des-Corbières **(8)** and Port-la-Nouvelle. There is little waymarking in either town.

POINTS OF INTEREST

Port-la-Nouvelle Still a working port, but also a seaside resort with a long, sandy beach. There is a good train service to the town. From mid-June to mid-September a *navette* bus runs from the station to the beach.

Wind Turbines An awesome line of 15 huge turbines. These modern, metallic constructions contrast with the old, abandoned stone buildings that are dotted around the plateau. From the hilltop, the view westwards extends over range upon range of the rolling, arid Corbières hills.

Roquefort-des-Corbières An attractive, prosperous-looking settlement backed by impressive limestone cliffs, topped by former windmills. Halfway up the Rue des Trois Moulins, in the centre of the town, there is a superb painting of the village on the wall of a house by a square.

Durban-Corbières The castle above the narrow, marble-paved streets of the town centre dates from the 11th century, but is not associated with the Cathars. It had no great military value for most if its life, and was more a sort of manor house. An historic monument with Renaissance window frames, it has been partially restored, although it is not open to the public at the time of writing (2005).

The castle at Durban-Corbières is not associated with the Cathars, but it has an interesting history and is being restored

STAGE 2
Durban-Corbières to Tuchan

Towards the end of this stage you at last reach your first Cathar castle – the hilltop fortress of Aguilar, an impressive sight.

This is a very long and exacting stage of the Sentier Cathare, the trail constantly climbing or descending, with at least four notable ascents. The landscape is not as arid as it is further east – vineyards and *garrigue* still dominate parts of the landscape, but there are also wide rivers and forests.

Embres-et-Castelmaure is the only village encountered on this stage. Although it is large, with handsome *bourgeois* houses, don't count on finding any shops or places to drink here – or anywhere else between Durban and Tuchan. Do carry plenty of water.

Distance	28km
Walking time	7 hours (plus at least half an hour to visit the remains of Aguilar Castle)
Altitude	Between 90m and 350m
Ascent/Descent	800m/730m
IGN 1:25,000 Maps	2547OT (Durban-Corbières Leucate) and 2447OT (Tuchan); Durban-Corbières is in map fold 3A of its map, Tuchan is in map fold 9C of its map

Navigation

Shortly after leaving Durban-Corbières, there are many twists and turns through vineyards, so follow the waymarks carefully.

The route down to Embres-et-Castelmaure (6) is easy to follow, but bear in mind that the latest 1:25,000 map (i.e. edition (2)) does not show the trail as going into that village.

From the centre of Durban-Corbières (1), head southwest along the D611, with the river on your right. Near the edge of the town, follow the waymarks into a tarmacked lane on the left.

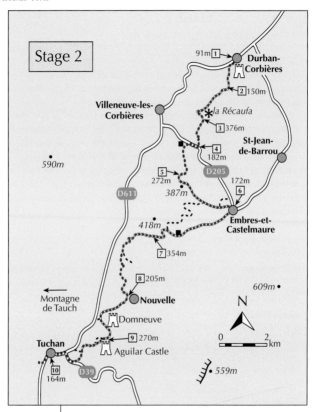

This lane winds up the hillside ahead, becomes a jeep track and reaches the Col de Sainte-Juste (**2**). There, turn right, descend, then turn left onto a path through the scrub. The path goes down to meet a track, which you follow until it reaches a stream and swings right. You then turn left onto a concrete track that climbs a hillside.

At a fork, turn left and follow an earth track between vineyards. You soon turn right, then left further on, and descend a little. Bear right at the bottom of the slope and follow the edge of a vineyard, soon to start climbing again. The tower you are aiming for (at la Récaufa) appears straight ahead, high above. At the top corner of the vineyard, take a path going into the low woodland on the right.

You now start a long, steep and possibly slippery climb, going straight ahead when you reach a path crossing en route. Not long after that, you cross stony ground, then swing to the left to tackle the final climb to the summit **(3)**. On your left is a stone monument topped with a statue of Sainte-Raphine. ▶

The route lies to the right of the monument – a clear track winding down steadily to the D205 **(4)**. Turn right and walk along the road for a few minutes (although if you want to reduce the length of this very long stage, you could turn left here and follow the D205 all the way to Embres-et-Castelmaure **(6)**). Where it bends distinctly to the right, take a wide jeep track going uphill on the half-left. This track climbs to the corner of a vineyard with a stone building on the right, then bends left. When it turns sharp right, go straight on, following a path into woodland ahead. The path follows the line of the valley bottom,

One of the finest views on this stage of the trail is from here. Durban-Corbières, with its château ruins, can be made out to the northeast, and Canigou mountain dominates the distant horizon to the southwest.

Embres-et-Castelmaure – sleepy but handsome

crossing the stream several times, eventually to climb away from the valley and into more open country.

When you reach a small col in open country (**5**), turn left. The path starts to climb steeply, and after some way, take a path on the left that contours around the side of the hill. On reaching a crossing with a track, turn left down that track, then bend to the right and follow the track beneath a vineyard on the right.

Keep to this track for some distance. It swings to the left and begins to descend a little, eventually joining another track coming in from the right. Turn left here and continue towards the lower ground ahead. ◀

The Sentier Cathare formerly went off to the right – you are about to follow a significant diversion of the route.

When the main track veers to the left, continue straight on, along a rougher track, which takes you down to the D205 again, where you turn right and immediately enter the village of Embres-et-Castelmaure (**6**). Continue on the road all the way through the village. Near the far end, where the main road turns to the left near a big wine *cave*, keep straight on along the Chemin de la Fontaine and emerge into open vineyard country again.

The lane climbs for some distance to reach a col, then descends and eventually reaches a stream, where the tarmac ends. Turn right here, cross the stream and follow the main track up the valley ahead. This track fords a couple of small streams and passes to the left of a restored stone building. You are now in a forest. On reaching a small open area, take the track on the far right and continue to climb up the valley ahead.

You soon join a substantial forest track at a sharp bend in that track – you are rejoining the former route of the Sentier Cathare. Continue straight ahead.

The track winds up the hillside, and views of the surrounding hills and valleys open up. At the Col de l'Ière (**7**) there is a meeting of tracks – go straight ahead to pick up a path through the scrub that descends into the valley on the other side of the col. At the bottom of the slope, the path meets a track, where you go left.

Swing right to cross a stream, then come to a distinct track fork. Go left here. The track zigzags steeply uphill and later starts a long traverse across the hillside.

After some distance, the slope levels out. Here, take a path on the right that plunges into the semi-woodland below. You now have a long, steady descent through scrub and semi-woodland. ▶ The path twice bends down into and crosses small valleys running down the hillside. Shortly after crossing the second stream course, the path rises to a small col, then goes down on the other side.

At various points from this path you may catch glimpses of Aguilar Castle on a prominent hill several kilometres to the south.

On reaching a fenced vineyard, go down its left-hand side. Continue down a track beyond the vineyard and, at the track fork below, go left. Just before reaching the outer buildings of Nouvelle **(8)**, turn right down a grass track to reach a tarmacked lane. Nouvelle, on the left, has one of the best-reputed wine *caves* in the region, but the sober Sentier Cathare turns right, in the opposite direction. The medieval tower and other remains at Nouvelle are not open to visitors.

Follow the lane down the valley ahead, and shortly before it reaches the D611, turn left onto another tarmacked lane, which immediately crosses a stream and

Vineyard scene near the end of Stage 2 (Aguilar Castle is on the far hilltop)

bends right. On the left is the crumbling ruin of a medieval château called Domneuve, but the lane bends left, after which you turn right onto a gravel track. At a fork shortly afterwards, go left and climb to a col.

From the col, **Aguilar Castle** now looms large on the hill directly ahead. After descending a short distance, the track meets a tarmacked lane **(9)**. To visit Aguilar, turn left into the car park, then ascend the hillside to the castle.

To continue along the Sentier Cathare, go down the tarmacked lane – the town of Tuchan on the lower ground ahead comes into view as you descend. After a short distance, turn sharp left onto a rough track that cuts off a loop in the tarmacked lane. Stay with that lane as it winds down onto the vineyard-covered plain below. At a T-junction of lanes turn left, and keep straight ahead until you reach the D39.

Turn right and walk alongside the D39 until it reaches an intersection with the D611. Turn left, and immediately after crossing a river, enter **Tuchan (10)**.

Notes for west–east walkers
The waymarking of the trail at the small col at point **(5)** may be a little unclear for west–east walkers. At the col, you turn **right**.

There are many track forks and path turnings to watch out for, especially in the last few kilometres before arriving at Durban-Corbières, so keep a constant eye open for the trail's waymarks.

POINTS OF INTEREST

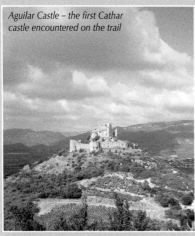
Aguilar Castle – the first Cathar castle encountered on the trail

Aguilar Castle The first of the Cathar castles on the Sentier Cathare, this hilltop fortress is surrounded by vineyards. To the west is the Montagne de Tauch, a high, steep-sided massif topped by wind turbines.

There has probably been a fortification on this site since Roman times, and the medieval fortress dates from at least the 11th century. Its Cathar-supporting owner was Raymond de Termes, who also controlled Termes Castle, 20km to the northwest. Termes Castle was seized by Simon de Montfort in 1210 after a siege that ended when rats infected the castle's water supply. The defenders were forced to flee, and most were caught and slaughtered, after which Aguilar Castle was taken without resistance. Like Termes, Aguilar was thus one of the first Cathar castles to fall to the French.

Raymond's son Olivier first fought against, then made submission to, the French king. In 1250 he regained Aguilar Castle, but a few years later it was sold back to the king. The castle was then substantially strengthened to help guard the new southern frontier of the French kingdom, becoming one of the 'five sons of Carcassonne' – that is, one of five castles that guarded Carcassonne against invasion from the south (the others were Puilaurens, Peyrepertuse, Quéribus and Termes), although in later centuries it lost its military significance and fell into ruin.

Today, a modest fee is charged for entrance to the castle ruins in the summer, but entry is free at other times.

Tuchan A pretty and unpretentious little town, Tulchan is clearly very proud of both its rugby team and the wine that is produced here. The heart of this ancient settlement was once fortified.

STAGE 3
Tuchan to Duilhac-sous-Peyrepertuse

Quéribus Castle lies on this stage of the trail. One of the most celebrated of the Cathar castles, it offers one of the most fantastic sights on the whole route.

Although this stage has only one significant climb (up to Quéribus Castle), it is a long and tough one.

Vineyards dominate the valleys and lower slopes of the landscape, while *garrigue* vegetation covers the high, craggy ground above the valleys. The limestone scenery is spectacular.

The trail passes through Cucugnan and Duilhac-sous-Peyrepertuse, which are particularly attractive villages.

Distance	23.5km
Walking time	6 hours 30 mins (plus an hour to visit Quéribus Castle)
Altitude	Between 160m and 600m (in addition, there is a climb of about 100m from the trail to Quéribus Castle)
Ascent/Descent	750m/560m
IGN 1:25,000 Map	2447OT (Tuchan); Tuchan is in map fold 9C, Duilhac-sous-Peyrepertuse is in map fold 5D

Navigation
The Molhet Priory (between (4) and (5)) is not shown on the IGN 1:25,000 map (edition 2).

The Sentier Cathare between Quéribus Castle (6) and Cucugnan (7) follows a steep descent, which could be especially slippery in wet conditions, so be very careful there. Alternatively, after visiting the castle, go back to the track junction at (5), and turn left to descend to Cucugnan by a less steep route – this is indicated by yellow waymarks. If you take this alternative route, add about half an hour to the walking time for this stage. Another option to avoid the very steep section is simply to follow the roads from the castle down to Cucugnan.

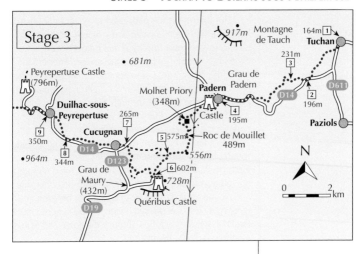

From the centre of Tuchan (**1**), near the church, take the road signposted 'D611 Paziols'. Follow that road southwards, out of the town, and when you reach a cemetery, turn right along a lane.

The lane comes into open country with vineyards all around. Carry straight on, onto a stony track, where the tarmac lane goes to the right. The trail then forks right and follows a footpath for a short distance before meeting another track, which ends at the entrance to a small vineyard. Turn left along this track, following it for some distance until you reach a fork under a small power line. Go left and soon emerge on the D14.

Turn right and follow the road for about 10 minutes. Then, with a small stone building on the left (**2**), turn right onto a track that climbs gently away from the road. The track bends to the left on reaching the foot of the craggy limestone pinnacles ahead. Fork left, then turn half-right up a rough enclosed path. Emerge onto another track and follow this as it swings to the right to cross a small ravine. At the end of the vineyard alongside which you have been walking, you come to the edge of another small ravine (**3**).

65

The long-distance path used to go straight ahead here, but has been washed away where it crosses the ravine, so you must turn right and follow a waymarked diversion around the head of the ravine. After coming down the other side, you meet the former path on the left. Go right here, and follow a delightful path contouring around the hillside through Mediterranean scrub.

The path turns sharp right where it goes around a rock spur, and here a marvellous new view comes into sight. In a limestone ridge you suddenly see a great cleft, formed by the River Verdouble – this cleft is called the Grau de Padern, and colossal boulders have tumbled down towards the riverbed from the cliffs on either side.

As you approach the Grau de Padern, the path, now quite stony, and steep-sided on the left, descends to meet the D14, which you follow through the gorge and across a bridge spanning the river.

You now have to follow the road for over a kilometre. There is a grass verge for much of the way, but be particularly careful on a narrow section, just after the bridge. To your right, high above, is the fluted cliff face of the Montagne de Tauch, looking like a collection of gargantuan limestone organ pipes. ◀

The prominently sited remains of Padern Castle come into view as you reach the outskirts of **Padern**.

Continue alongside the main road, with the river on your right (an alternative route for horse riders goes up a lane on the left and avoids the centre of the village). On reaching the Placette de l'Église, in the centre of the village **(4)**, turn left and follow a paved path around the right of a small church. Turn left on reaching a narrow tarmacked lane, then almost immediately turn right and climb another paved path up to the top of the village. Above, on your right, is a charming little chapel. At the end of a concrete lane, turn right onto a path that winds up the hillside. Turn right onto a second path and you soon come to a col. The remains of **Padern Castle** are on the right.

Go straight ahead onto a wide, well-surfaced track that gradually descends. Where this track veers right, near the bottom, take an unsurfaced jeep track going uphill, almost straight ahead. This track goes underneath

Padern village and castle, on Stage 3 of the Sentier Cathare, as seen from the River Verdouble

a major power line and passes, on the left, some bee-hives. When it descends to a track fork, go left. You now have a long, stiff climb ahead, as the track ascends alongside vineyards, curls to the left and ends. Here, you go straight ahead onto a footpath which, after a couple of sharp turns, passes just below **Molhet Priory** (on the left).

The path bears to the right and climbs the spur of the hill ahead. The village of Cucugnan is below, on the right, and beyond, on the far horizon, is the precipitous ridge on which the remains of Peyrepertuse Castle are perched.

After a long haul, you emerge onto a forest track. Turn right and follow the track uphill to a patch of flat, open ground. The Sentier Cathare turns sharp left, con-tinuing along the same track. On the right is the Roc de Mouillet, an excellent viewpoint.

The track soon swings sharply to the right. After a stiff climb up the winding track, you at last emerge onto the other side of the ridge. From here on, Quéribus Castle, mightily impressive on its eagle's-nest perch, comes into view.

A little further on, the Sentier Cathare waymarks take you on a U-shaped route around a spur at 556m. About 500m further on, the route turns left **(5)**. (The track going straight ahead offers the alternative, less steep route down to Cucugnan – see above.)

The trail terraces around the hillside to arrive at a ticket office **(6)** at the foot of the pinnacle on which sits **Quéribus Castle**.

After visiting the castle and returning to the ticket office, go up the hill opposite, where visitors' cars are parked. After winding through the scrub at the top of this hill, the path turns left and starts the long, steep and potentially very slippery descent towards Cucugnan. Further down, the path bears right and descends an open section where the soil is almost red in colour (this is a relatively recent short diversion). The trail then comes down into a valley where it meets a track and turns right.

The trail descends abruptly between Quéribus and Cucugnan (in the distance)

Duilhac village and Peyrepertuse Castle high above

Cross a stream and rise to meet a tarmacked lane by some cypress trees. Turn left here. The lane bears right and reaches a crossing where you turn left to go up to the D14 **(7)**. Cross that road, then climb the hill ahead to enter **Cucugnan**.

Go through the village. At the far end, after passing a windmill above on the right and a restaurant on the left, the waymarking may be a little confusing. Go down to the D14 and turn right for a few metres along that road, passing in front of a tourist office, then fork right, down a narrow tarmacked lane.

After a short distance along this lane, you come to a fork. Go right, then follow the lane ahead for well over a kilometre, as it passes through an area covered mostly by vineyards. Eventually this lane rejoins the D14 **(8)**, where you turn right and walk alongside the road for a short distance.

Turn right, down a waymarked track. Ahead, Duilhac-sous-Peyrepertuse, and behind and above it Peyrepertuse Castle, form a highly photogenic landscape. Where the track bends left and is about to become a tarmacked lane, turn off onto another track on the right. This descends, weaves about a little and is joined by others from time to time. Where it approaches a stream, go right, then left and cross the stream.

When you reach a crossing of tarmacked lanes, go straight ahead. After a little way, fork left onto a narrower lane, then left again onto a dirt track, weaving up a slope to eventually join the D14 again. Turn right and follow the road through the lower part of **Duilhac-sous-Peyrepertuse (9)**. This takes you to the Auberge de la Source, situated by a magnificent spring.

Padern Village and Castle The village is squeezed between the wide River Verdouble (a fearsome sight during periods of heavy rainfall) and the steep slope on which sit the impressive castle remains. The castle has only slender links with the Cathar period, and was in any case completely rebuilt in the 17th century. It is now as ruined as castles constructed centuries earlier.

Molhet Priory The remains of this medieval fortified priory are scant, but merit a respectful pause. The stone carving that has survived was evidently sculpted with skill.

Quéribus Castle Quéribus Castle is said to be the last of the Cathar strongholds. In 1255, the defender of Quéribus was a fervent Cathar supporter – one Chabert de Barbaira. He had long since been dispossessed of his property in Languedoc by the crusade, but he himself survived, took to the hills, established Quéribus as his base, and for over 20 years took part in guerrilla raids on French troops to the north.

The French were naturally eager to prise de Barbaira out of Quéribus, but despite their huge military strength in the region, they found it no easy task. A siege of the castle in 1248 ended in failure, and it was not until seven years later that Quéribus finally fell.

Soon afterwards the castle was strengthened by the French king, becoming a key frontier fortress, due to its position so very close to the border with Spain. It was the scene of fighting in the 15th century, and for a while was once again held by the Spanish, but after the 17th century, when the frontier moved well to the south, the castle was left to crumble. Fortunately, much of the fortifications remain, and Quéribus now presents one of the most awe-inspiring sights in Cathar castle country. The whole structure is surprisingly large, given how little ground there is to build anything on.

Inside there is some well-preserved vaulting, and from the top of the tower there is one of the most stunning panoramas in Cathar castle country – the coast is far to the east, and Canigou mountain rises majestically to the south.

The castle is closed for much of January, but otherwise open throughout the year, although it sometimes closes at short notice if the wind becomes so strong that walking around the castle is judged to be dangerous. The entry ticket to the castle also gives free entry to the theatre in Cucugnan.

Quéribus Castle

POINTS OF INTEREST

Cucugnan This attractive village has benefited perhaps more than any other from being close to Cathar castles. Mostly free of traffic, it has craft shops, a neo-Gothic church, and a restored windmill. There is also the tiny Théâtre Achille Mir, named after a local 19th-century writer. He wrote a story in Occitan of a sermon about hellfire and damnation given by the *curé* of Cucugnan to his wayward, pleasure-loving flock. Alphonse Daudet subsequently wrote a French version of the story that is widely known in France, and an intriguing 20-minute presentation of the story, in French, is shown in the theatre. There are continuous performances throughout the year, except in January.

Duilhac-sous-Peyrepertuse This village has several attractive features, including its restored church, once part of a small medieval fort, and the Auberge de la Source, which is in a former olive oil mill. But most striking of all is the powerful spring that emerges from a rock face next to the auberge. From its several outlets, delicious fresh water tumbles into a canal.

Notes for west–east walkers
There are innumerable path turnings and forks to watch out for on this section of the trail, especially immediately after leaving Duilhac-sous-Peyrepertuse, on the section through Padern, and across the vineyard-covered approach to Tuchan, although they are all well waymarked.

Be particularly watchful also when approaching two recent diversions – one between Cucugnan and Quéribus, the other just before point **(3)**.

STAGE 4 (MAIN ROUTE)

Duilhac-sous-Peyrepertuse to Prugnanes

This stage begins with a long climb, dominated by the huge, towering cliffs on which stand the ruins of Peyrepertuse Castle, the largest of the Cathar castles, apart from Foix and Carcassonne. To visit Peyrepertuse, you must turn off the trail for a short distance, and you should allow a couple of hours for this detour and a tour of the castle.

Later on this stage, you approach the stunning Galamus Gorge, but the Main Route of the trail does not go through the gorge itself (the North Variant does). Instead, the Main Route descends and crosses the River Agly, then climbs over a hill to the village of Prugnanes.

The landscape continues as scrub-covered limestone hills, with steep crags and deep ravines. Vineyards become more scattered, and there are extensive views over the Fenouillèdes Hills to the south.

Distance	17.5km
Walking time	4 hours 30 mins (plus two hours to visit Peyrepertuse Castle)
Altitude	Between 280m and 670m
Ascent/Descent	650m/670m (in addition, there is a climb of about 200m from the trail to Peyrepertuse Castle)
IGN 1:25,000 Map	2447OT (Tuchan); Duilhac-sous-Peyrepertuse is in map fold 5D, Prugnanes is in map fold 1D

Navigation

Much of this section of the Sentier Cathare – from point **(2)** to point **(8)** – follows the same route as that of the GR36 long-distance path, so you will see red and white waymarks as well as the Sentier Cathare's blue and yellow ones.

Near the entrance to the Galamus Gorge, at point **(5)**, the Main Route goes down into the Agly Valley, while the North Variant continues along the road through the gorge.

The area crossed by this stage is rich in local walking routes that carry yellow waymarks and occasional homemade signs – be careful not to wander off onto one of these local circuits.

Climb up through Duilhac-sous-Peyrepertuse (1) and emerge onto the tarmacked access road to **Peyrepertuse Castle**.

The Sentier Cathare climbs the winding access road for a couple of kilometres, with the castle perched on the massive cliffs to the right.

You eventually reach a point (2) where the access road to the castle swings sharply to the right, while the Sentier Cathare continues straight on, along a jeep track heading west. (To visit the castle, turn right here, and return to this point later.)

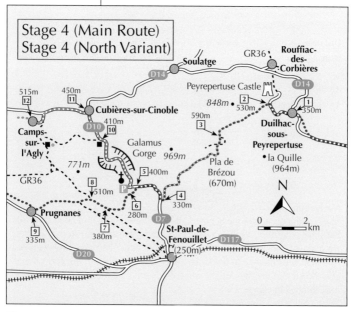

Follow the track ahead, as it terraces high above the valley on your left, for 2.5km. At the head of that valley, the track bends to the left. To the right is a view of the Pech de Bugarach.

Fork right off the track, along a path that goes through a gap in a fence **(3)**.

Terrace around the head of a valley, falling away to the right. The path joins a track on the left. Turn right along that track for a very few metres, then left, off the track, and pass below a watering point for livestock.

The path now enters woodland and climbs stiffly beneath limestone crags, finally emerging onto an open plateau, the Pla de Brézou.

The trail crosses the plateau, descending gently, then enters woodland and descends into a valley. The surface becomes rocky, and perhaps a little slippery, and you then enter relatively open country, the path swinging left around the shoulder of a hill.

At the Col de Corbasse the path swings right, descending quite steeply straight down a small valley. Finally, you cross a stream where there is a small vineyard on the right. You are now on a jeep track that later swings to the right and descends to meet the D7 **(4)**.

St-Paul-de-Fenouillet and, beyond, the Galamus Gorge; the trail runs from right to left, along the high ground, before descending to the gorge, where the Main Route of the trail continues to the west (to the left), and the North Variant goes through the gorge itself

If you want to go to **St-Paul-de-Fenouillet** from here, turn left down the D7 (although you might like first to turn right to view the Galamus Gorge – see below). To return to the trail from St-Paul, follow one of the various possible routes by road, track or path that are marked on the 1:25,000 map. For example, take the lane that branches north off the D117 on the western outskirts of St-Paul, near the Champion supermarket. After crossing the railway line, it is signposted for walkers and cyclists as a route to Palmières. From there, head west along a track to Prugnanes, meeting the Main Route of the Sentier Cathare along the way.

From **(4)**, the Main Route turns right and follows the D7 uphill for a couple of kilometres.

At **(5)**, where there is a sign for a car park 200m beyond, the Main Route turns sharp left down a stony path, and the North Variant continues along the road.

From the car park there is a view of the magnificent Galamus Gorge, and a famous hermitage perched on

The entrance to the Galamus Gorge; the buildings clinging to the lower part of the cliff on the right are those of the medieval hermitage of St-Antoine-de-Galamus

one of its cliffs, so it worth walking up to the car park and back to admire the view before you go down the path.

The path from **(5)** descends steeply into the valley, zigzagging at first. After those zigzags, go right at a path fork. Eventually, you arrive at the bottom of the valley, by a small canal. A large building (la Tirounère) can be seen on the other side of the wide River Agly. Cross the river here by a wooden footbridge **(6)**.

Turn left up a wide track. If a gate ahead is locked, pass through a gap to the right of it. The tarmacked lane beyond the gate rises to a small col where you turn right, onto a jeep track. Where the track swings left, go straight on, onto a footpath leading into the semi-woodland beyond.

The path starts to climb steeply. Eventually it comes to a T-junction of paths at the Col de Lenti **(7)**, where you turn right. (After a few metres, a path goes off to the left – it used to be signposted for Prugnanes, but this is no

Fit-looking French hikers on the trail – the red book is the French guide to the Sentier Cathare

longer the case, although it is evidently still well used. It soon descends to meet a track that, to the right, eventually reaches Prugnanes. The official route of the Sentier Cathare is rather longer, and is described in the following paragraph.)

Beyond the Col de Lenti, the path zigzags up a section of dark, craggy rock, then comes to a path fork **(8)**. Turn left and follow the path into the valley below. (The GR36 continues straight ahead, up the slope.) In the bottom of the valley, join a track and turn right along it. The track climbs a little, then descends gently to **Prugnanes (9)**.

Notes for west–east walkers

If you want to go to **St-Paul-de-Fenouillet**, follow one of the various possible routes by road, track or path that lead off the trail and that are marked on the 1:25,000 map. For example, take the path that is signposted from the Col de Lenti **(7)** to St Paul. After passing through a pine forest, this route descends to the town on a jeep track running past vineyards. The shortest way back to the trail from St Paul is up the D7. You meet the trail at point **(4)**.

After crossing the River Agly, the trail climbs steeply to the D7. Be careful not to take another path that forks to the right and goes past a metal seat.

POINTS OF INTEREST

Peyrepertuse Castle This castle was another bastion of Cathar support, and its occupant, Guilhem de Peyrepertuse, was excommunicated by the Pope for his opposition to the crusade. However, the castle's remote location and formidable natural defences long dissuaded French military leaders from trying to take it by force.

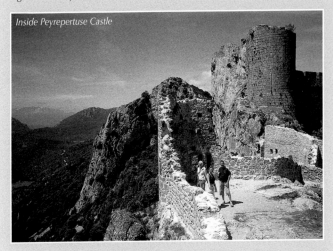

Inside Peyrepertuse Castle

But in 1240 Guilhem de Peyrepertuse took part in an audacious attempt to recover Carcassonne from the French. When that attempt failed, the assailants fled southwards towards the Pyrenees. French troops pursued them and, in so doing, laid siege to Peyrepertuse. Caught at the beginning of winter without supplies or hope of receiving military support, Guilhem de Peyrepertuse surrendered the castle to the French.

The Treaty of Corbeil, between Louis IX of France and Jaume I of Aragon, was signed in 1258. It was drawn up to establish a clear frontier across a region that the two powers had fought over for generations. It also sealed the victory of France in its campaign to seize control of Languedoc – a campaign that had effectively begun nearly 50 years earlier with the massacre at Béziers. →

→ The new frontier, running westwards from the Mediterranean coast near Rivesaltes, placed Peyrepertuse Castle just a few kilometres on the French side. It became a royal fortress, part of the chain of French castles along the frontier, and was almost completely rebuilt.

When the frontier moved further south in the 17th century, Peyrepertuse lost its military significance and fell into ruin, but was designated an historic monument in 1908. Since 1977 it has been the site of important archaeological investigations, so famous that it appeared on a French postage stamp in 2004.

The buildings and walls of this castle are strung out along a limestone ridge with steep cliffs on nearly all sides. From a distance, the ridge looks like part of a gigantic fossil jawbone, with a monstrous isolated molar tooth at one end. The leading Cathar historian Michel Roquebert has described Peyrepertuse as a 'petite Carcassonne céleste' – a small Carcassonne, high in the sky.

The castle is open every day throughout the year, except in January. It may be closed at short notice in stormy conditions.

St-Paul-de-Fenouillet This is the largest settlement on or near the trail between Port-la-Nouvelle and Quillan. A centuries-old town, it has an impressive *chapitre*, a former wealthy collegiate church. This historic monument, which is now being restored, houses a local history museum.

Prugnanes A charming village, off the main tourist trails, there are no shops, but the water from the fountain in the village centre is drinkable, and the *gîte d'étape* sells food and drink.

STAGE 4 (NORTH VARIANT)

Duilhac-sous-Peyrepertuse to Camps-sur-l'Agly

This variant passes through the amazing Galamus Gorge, one of the most striking landscape features along the whole trail.

The route of this variant between points **(1)** and **(5)** is as for Stage 4 (Main Route).

From point **(5)**, all the way to Camps-sur-l'Agly **(12)**, the North Variant follows roads. However, there is an unofficial off-road alternative from the northern end of the gorge to Camps-sur-l'Agly.

Beyond the gorge, the countryside takes on a distinctly more pastoral appearance.

See the sketch map accompanying Stage 4, Main Route.

Distance	19km
Walking time	5 hours (plus 2 hours to visit Peyrepertuse Castle)
Altitude	Between 330m and 670m
Ascent/Descent	560m/400m (in addition, there is a climb of about 200m from the trail to Peyrepertuse Castle)
IGN 1:25,000 Map	2447OT (Tuchan); Duilhac-sous-Peyrepertuse is in map fold 5D, Camps-sur-l'Agly is in map fold 1D

Navigation

Please read the navigation notes for Stage 4 (Main Route).

The alternative route starts just past an old mill on the Galamus Gorge road. Although not indicated by Sentier Cathare waymarks, it is well used and carries other signs and waymarks along the way.

Follow Stage 4 of the Main Route of the trail from Duilhac-sous-Peyrepertuse **(1)** as far as the entrance to the Galamus Gorge **(5)**.

From the car park facing the **Galamus Gorge**, walk along the D7 going north through the gorge (watch out for traffic approaching from both directions).

The upper part of the Galamus Gorge has rock pools, into which youngsters plunge from a great height

Towards the head of the gorge, the road (now the D10) and the riverbed approach the same level. Below are rock pools where people bathe on hot days. Eventually the valley widens out again. The road passes, on the left, a building by the river that was once a medieval mill, and is now a bar–restaurant.

Where the road bends to the right, about 200m after passing the old mill, there is a path going down on the left **(10)**. This is the start of the alternative, informal off-road route to Camps-sur-l'Agly, described below.

The Sentier Cathare proper continues along the road to the village of **Cubières-sur-Cinoble (11)**. There, at a T-junction, turn left onto the D14, and follow it as it winds through the semi-wooded countryside. After about 2km, turn left onto the access road signposted for the village of Camps-sur-l'Agly. Cross a stream, wind up a hillside and enter Camps-sur-l'Agly **(12)**.

The *gîte d'étape*, La Ferme de Camps, is at the far end of the village, but if you are staying overnight at the *gîte d'étape* in la Bastide, you must carry on for another 2.5km, on Stage 5 of this North Variant.

Alternative Route to Camps-sur-l'Agly from (10)

After turning left off the D10, just beyond the old mill, the alternative route crosses an irrigation canal and then a stream. After crossing a small meadow, it then reaches the River Agly. Cross the river there if you can (if not, go upstream to a footbridge), and turn right to follow the path on the other side of the river.

After walking for about a kilometre through woodland on the riverbank, follow a path to the left, away from the river. (Other paths go off in various directions, so follow the signposts for Camps.)

There is then a long climb, mainly in woodland. Near the top of the slope, go right at a path fork. Beyond, at a col on open ground, go straight ahead and follow the grass track opposite. It descends, goes past a small lake on the left, then rises to meet a jeep track. Turn right and follow the jeep track. It descends, crosses a stream, then rises to enter Camps-sur-l'Agly.

Camps-sur-l'Agly, at the western end of the North Variant of Stage 4

POINTS OF INTEREST

The Galamus Gorge The River Agly has scythed a cleft some 400m deep into a limestone ridge, and the gorge is a breathtaking sight. The road through it, carved into the near-vertical eastern cliff, was constructed in 1894. Canyoners love the gorge – you may hear people below, their voices echoing in the ravine, as they swim and slither along the riverbed.

The hermitage of St-Antoine-de-Galamus (a chapel in a cave and a couple of buildings clinging to a ledge in the cliff) is visible from the car park at the southern end of the gorge, and can be reached by a short but spectacular footpath from that car park. It was occupied by the Franciscans in medieval times and is still a place of pilgrimage.

You can buy drinks at the hermitage in July and August. Also during that period, traffic along the road through the gorge is controlled, so that at any one time it is only moving in one direction.

Cubières-sur-Cinoble There was a large abbey here in medieval times, but the village's curiously shaped church is almost all that is left of it. Cubières was also the home of Bélibaste, the last of the Cathar 'Bons Hommes' in Languedoc. He was burnt at the stake in 1321.

STAGE 5 (MAIN ROUTE)
Prugnanes to Puilaurens

On this stage, the trail runs beneath the remains of the so-called Fenouillet castles, probably the least known of the fortresses associated with the Cathars, but striking and interesting features that are well worth visiting.

Near the end of this stage, the commanding Cathar castle of Puilaurens suddenly comes into view.

This stage also passes through the handsome town of Caudiès-de-Fenouillèdes, crosses a wide synclinal basin that has been a major feature of the landscape south of the trail since you reached Quéribus, then goes through the impressive Saint-Jaume Gorge.

Limestone hills and crags continue to loom up on all sides, but the vineyards end and forests start to dominate the landscape.

For accommodation, you may wish to stay at the Aigues-Bonnes *gîte d'étape*, which nestles in the hills 3km before the trail reaches Puilaurens. Otherwise, you will need to seek lodgings a little way to the north or the south of that village.

Distance	18.5km
Walking time	4 hours 45 mins (allow also about one and a half hours to reach and visit the Fenouillet castles, and half an hour to walk from Puilaurens to Lapradelle if you seek accommodation in Lapradelle)
Altitude	Between 335m and 690m
Ascent/Descent	450m/330m (in addition, there is a climb of about 150m to visit the Fenouillet castles)
IGN 1:25,000 Map	2348ET (Prades); Prugnanes is in map fold 3A, Puilaurens is in map fold 1B

Navigation

The trail coincides with the route of the GR36 long-distance path from Caudiès **(3)** to near the Fenouillet castles, so red and white waymarks appear along this section of the trail. Red and yellow waymarks are also seen, e.g. at les Bordes **(4)**, just beyond the Saint-Jaume gorge. These denote the route of the Tour du Fenouillèdes regional path.

Also at Les Bordes, a horse-riders' alternative route for the Sentier Cathare turns off the main route and heads south to a *gîte d'étape* at a place called the Col de Tulla. This alternative route is not described here, but it is waymarked orange and rejoins the main Sentier Cathare at the col at 689m **(5)**, just west of Aigues-Bonnes.

At the northern end of Prugnanes **(1)**, take the lane that forks to the left. It becomes an unsurfaced track and passes through countryside covered in vineyards.

Join the D20, turn sharp right, and walk along it for some distance. On reaching a col, turn right onto a track **(2)**. This track becomes a fine balcony route.

Later, there is a succession of track junctions – go straight ahead each time. As the dark-surfaced trail runs gently downhill, with pine trees covering nearby hillsides, **Caudiès-de-Fenouillèdes** comes into view in the vineyard-covered valley below. The track becomes tarmacked as it starts to cross the valley.

Join the D20 from Prugnanes again. Not long afterwards, cross a bridge over the Boulzane river and enter Caudiès **(3)**. Here the trail turns left, climbs up the eastern edge of the town and reaches the D117 (the centre of the town is on the right).

Cross the busy D117 into the Avenue de l'Ermitage, which soon crosses a railway line and takes you out of Caudiès. Almost immediately after passing, on the left, an olive tree planted by children from Mostar in the Balkans, fork right onto a lane heading south.

The lane passes what are the last vineyards you will probably see on the trail. After a pair of stone pillars, fork left. The track becomes a footpath, enters low woodland and climbs a little.

When the path emerges onto a jeep track, turn left and follow the track downhill. At a wide junction of tracks, take the track in the middle. The trail continues to

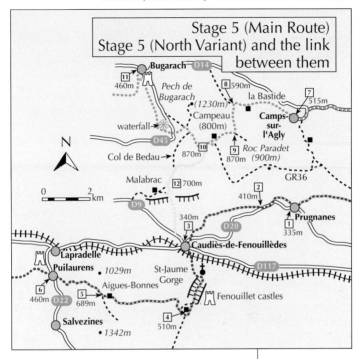

descend and follows a lovely avenue, bordered by pine trees. At the bottom of the hill, you reach a shady picnic area. The chapel of Notre Dame de Laval is up on the left, its magnificent oak door, with elaborate ironwork, recently restored by local craftsmen.

At the far end of the picnic site, turn right along the D9 and follow it for about 200m. Where the road bends left to cross a river, go straight ahead onto a footpath.

That path enters the **Saint-Jaume Gorge**. There are handrails along the more exposed sections, and you cross a number of concrete footbridges.

Beyond the gorge, the path approaches a waterfall. There you cross the river over another footbridge and follow a path up to a tarmacked lane.

The Sentier Cathare passes through the St-Jaume Gorge

Turn left along the lane for a few metres and reach a road junction. The trail goes right here, but to visit the **Fenouillet castles**, leave the Sentier Cathare for now and follow the GR36 across the bridge on the left. It climbs to la Vilasse (one of a number of hamlets in the commune of Fenouillet). The two castles are above and on either side of that hamlet.

Return to the road junction and follow the Sentier Cathare up the road. Go between two stone buildings and, shortly after the road bends to the left, take a footpath on the right that climbs a steep, partly wooded slope. Behind, there is a fine view across the valley to the Fenouillet castles.

The path reaches the hamlet of les Bordes **(4)** – there is a signposted drinking water tap on the left. Pass through the hamlet and reach a tarmacked road. Turn right here (the horse-riders' alternative route and the Tour du Fenouillèdes go to the left). After descending for a short distance along this road, fork left onto a lane.

The lane bears right, then climbs to the left around the spur of a hill. Where the track forks, go right. The lane now climbs steadily westwards, up the long Aigues-Bonnes Valley. At first you pass through semi-open country, then enter a forest higher up. Eventually you reach a col, with a distinctive conical hill on the right. The trail bears right and descends, soon to reach the Aigues-Bonnes *gîte d'étape*.

There is then a steep, winding climb up a track to another col at 689m **(5)**. On the way up there are fine views back down the valley. At the col, the horse-riders' alternative route joins on the left. Thereafter you begin a descent to Puilaurens in a deep valley.

As the track winds down the hill, the landscape opens out, steep limestone cliffs soaring on either side. Lower down, Puilaurens Castle, perched on an isolated hill, suddenly appears. This is a grand section of the trail.

Finally, the trail enters **Puilaurens (6)**. It crosses a river and reaches the D22.

There is currently no accommodation in Puilaurens itself, but accommodation can be found in Lapradelle

In Puilaurens, at the end of Stage 5 of the Main Route

(about 1km to the north, along the D22), and at a bed and breakfast – the Mas Occitan – just south of Puilaurens.

Notes for west–east walkers

Soon after passing through les Bordes **(4)** and going downhill, you join the GR36 long-distance path by a road bridge. There, be careful to pick up the path that goes down into the Saint-Jaume Gorge.

On the section from Caudiès **(3)** to Prugnanes **(1)** there are several forks and turnings to look out for.

POINTS OF INTEREST

Caudiès-de-Fenouillèdes A formerly fortified settlement which has some attractive buildings – in particular, timber-framed houses in the central square – Caudiès-de-Fenouillèdes also has several shops.

The Saint-Jaume Gorge Though not nearly as deep as the Galamus Gorge, this is a marvellous chasm to walk through, and is on a popular local walk. The walls of the gorge form a natural rock garden, with wild flowers and delicate ferns in almost every crevice.

The Fenouillet Castles Up to the middle of the 13th century, these fortresses were occupied by Cathar supporters, before being confiscated by the French king. The Château St Pierre, immediately to the north of la Vilasse, was a

The two Fenouillet castles, as seen from the trail

sizeable fortified settlement. The hilltop site is completely open and access to the ruins is currently without charge. From here, you look over the hills crossed by the gorge, and across the beautiful landscape of woods and vineyards in which lie the chapel of Notre Dame de Laval and Caudiès-de-Fenouillèdes. The Pech de Bugarach towers above everything to the north. The clifftop ruins of the lookout castle to the south of la Vilasse – the Castel Sabordas – can be reached by a lane that passes to the right of the village cemetery. A short way along that lane, turn right onto a track that leads to the castle. Be careful here – the ruins are on an exposed site – but the view is stunning.

Puilaurens A pretty little riverside settlement, with Puilaurens Castle directly above it. The French Resistance was active around here, and in August 1944 American troops parachuted onto nearby hillsides and began the liberation of this part of Aude. There is a monument to their bravery in the village of Salvezines, a couple of kilometres south of Puilaurens.

STAGE 5 (NORTH VARIANT)
Camps-sur-l'Agly to Bugarach

This is the shortest of all the stages of the Sentier Cathare. It consists of a long climb up to a ridge at an altitude of about 910m, just above the Col de Péchines **(9)**, followed by a long descent. The ridge offers an excellent viewpoint.

Between the two ends of this stage there is only one settlement – the hamlet of la Bastide. Most of the isolated buildings that you pass are uninhabited and in a state of ruin.

Pastureland, woodland and scrub predominate, and a beech wood below the Pech de Bugarach is another indication that Atlantic influences are taking over from Mediterranean ones.

The trail curves around the eastern and southern flanks of the magnificent Pech de Bugarach, but does not go to the summit.

There are no Cathar castles on this stage, but the Cascade des Mathieux is a pretty waterfall, and possibly the only signposted *cascade* along the trail.

See the sketch map accompanying Stage 5 (Main Route).

Distance	12km
Walking time	3 hours 45 mins (plus about half an hour if you leave the trail for a while to see the Cascade des Mathieux)
Altitude	Between 460m and 910m
Ascent/Descent	500m/560m
IGN 1:25,000 Map	2347OT (Quillan); Camps-sur-l'Agly is in map fold 10D, Bugarach is in map fold 8C

Navigation
On a short section from Campeau to la Couillade **(10)**, this stage follows the same route as the GR36 long-distance path, so you will see red and white waymarks along that section.

At la Couillade **(10)**, you fork right for Bugarach. The route to the left goes down to Caudiès-de-Fenouillèdes and offers a link back to the Main Route (see the next stage, Stage 5, Link from North Variant to Main Route).

On reaching the D45, the walkers' route of the trail goes straight ahead and soon fords a river. After heavy rain the river may be difficult or impossible to cross, so walkers should return a little way and go down the D45 instead. That route is described below. For most of the way it is waymarked orange, as a horse-riders' alternative route to Bugarach.

To reach the Cascade des Mathieux from the trail, you have to scramble down a very steep and possibly slippery slope. Be especially careful when the ground is wet.

The Sentier Cathare leaves Camps-sur-l'Agly **(7)** at its western end, just beyond the *gîte d'étape*. Take a track going down to the left, descending gently to the River Agly. Cross the river by a footbridge, on the right. After picking up the track again on the other side, you quickly meet a tarmacked lane. Turn left along that lane.

The lane heads west, taking you through what is mostly open countryside. It also brings you ever closer to the magnificent, buttressed east face of the Pech de Bugarach. You eventually enter the hamlet of la Bastide,

The Sentier Cathare passes close to the imposing east face of the Pech de Bugarach

whose stone buildings, some crumbling and some restored, are impressive in scale. (There is also a *gîte d'étape* here.)

Continue along the tarmacked lane, beyond la Bastide, and after about 600m turn left **(8)** onto a track that takes you across semi-open ground. This is the beginning of what is going to be a long and hard climb up the hillside ahead. Where you meet another track, turn left. The track climbs into woodland, then zigzags a little (the Pech de Bugarach is now behind you).

On eventually reaching more open ground, the trail swings sharply to the right, and at first its line may not be too evident. You enter a woodland of box and beech trees, and the slope becomes very steep.

After a slog up the winding path, you emerge onto an open ridge. A pause here is irresistible – on a clear day the panorama is superb. The rolling Fenouillèdes Hills are to the south, with mountains of the eastern Pyrenees beyond; the Pech de Bugarach looms up close by on the right, and the dry, rough-edged hills of Corbières roll away to the north. As for Cathar castles, look carefully and you may be able to pick out, about 10km to the southwest, the bastion of Puilaurens perched on an isolated hill.

Descend the slope beyond the ridge, passing through a belt of trees, to reach a col where the ruins of a building on the right are being engulfed in vegetation – this is the Col de Péchines **(9)**. Follow a path that goes down to the right. This path bears to the left as it descends, and then enters a wide basin of open land.

At the bottom you reach the sizeable ruins of Campeau, one of the most idyllic locations along the trail, situated far from any road or settlement. The remains of the former farmstead are almost hidden among trees, nestling by a well at the head of a broad valley. The surrounding extensive pastureland was once a significant cereal-growing area.

With Campeau behind you, the route now goes to the right of the nearby small artificial lake. A few metres from the ruins, pass by a stone shelter which houses the

Descending at a brisk pace on the trail below the Pech de Bugarach

The Cascade des Mathieux

old well. Go up the slope over semi-open ground ahead, then meet and follow to the left a faintly defined track for a short distance. You are now in open pastureland with a steep slope to the left. Turn left and go straight up that slope, past some piles of stones and towards the top corner of the pasture. Here, go through a short stretch of wooded land to pass, on the right, the ruins of the Bergerie de la Couillade **(10)**.

Turn right and go uphill on a footpath to emerge onto a track again. Turn left onto this track and immediately reach a col, where a completely new vista opens out. The track soon turns sharp right, then goes downhill for some way through a beech wood. At the bottom of the slope, leave the track where it bears left and go straight ahead onto a path climbing up through more woodland.

You soon emerge onto open ground, with the colossal cliffs of the Pech de Bugarach on the right. The path now traverses the semi-wooded hillside for some distance. Eventually, a path goes off to the right, signposted for the *fenêtre* (a natural 'window' in a rock face) and the summit of the **Pech de Bugarach**. Carry straight on, and shortly afterwards reach another path fork where you descend to the left.

Lower down, you meet the D45. The trail goes across the road, through a gate, and then descends to the right, going through woodland to a river crossing.

(If the river is too difficult to cross – and bear in mind that you would have to cross it again later – go back up to the road, turn left and follow it towards Bugarach. After nearly 2km, watch out for where a track forks left off the road, and goes downhill alongside a small power line. Take that track. At the bottom of the slope, cross a stream, meet a track and turn right. You have now rejoined the walkers' trail.)

If you crossed the river just below the D45, bear right. Soon afterwards an off-trail path on the right is signposted to the Cascade des Mathieux. If conditions allow – that is, if the ground underfoot is not too wet and slippery – descend to admire this splendid waterfall.

Back on the trail, you are now on a track heading roughly northwards. After rounding a rocky spur, the track traverses the hillside, with impressive views to the right towards the crags of the Pech de Bugarach and into the deep valley below.

Eventually the track descends again to the river and crosses it. Beyond is a lake. Go alongside the right-hand edge of the lake, then follow the track beyond it as far as the D14.

The 1000-year-old village of Bugarach (11), with its crumbling 16th-century château, lies straight ahead.

Notes for west–east walkers

Be especially careful not to lose the trail between the col just above the Bergerie de la Couillade (10) and Campeau.

Take care also at the Col de Péchines (9). There, turn left to climb the path up a steep slope that leads to the crest of a ridge. The trail then descends steeply through box woodland on the other side.

POINTS OF INTEREST

Pech de Bugarach This peak, surrounded by huge cliffs on almost all sides, and rising to over 1200m, has been compared to Ayers Rock in Australia. It can be seen from far away and from several stages of the trail.

However, it is not advisable to climb the *fenêtre* route from the Sentier Cathare while carrying a heavy backpack. If you want to climb this peak, spend an extra night in the area, devote a separate day to that walk, and go out with a small daypack. There are waymarked routes to the summit from, for example, Bugarach, as described in my earlier book, *Walks in the Cathar Region* (Cicerone, 2005).

STAGE 5
Link from North Variant to Main Route

This is a link from the North Variant back to the Main Route, leaving the North Variant at the Bergerie de la Couillade (10) and joining the Main Route at Caudiès-de-Fenouillèdes (3).

The main advantages of using this link are described in the introduction.

This link takes you over an especially beautiful, high, open plateau near the Col del Bedau.

See the sketch map accompanying Stage 5 (Main Route).

Distance	7 km, making the whole distance on Stage 5, from Camps-sur-l'Agly to Puilaurens, 25.6km (13.7km to Caudiès-de-Fenouillèdes, then 11.9km from there to Puilaurens)
Walking time	1 hour 45 mins, making the whole walking time on Stage 5, from Camps-sur-l'Agly to Puilaurens, 7 hours 15 mins (4 hours to Caudiès-de-Fenouillèdes, then 3 hours 15 mins from there to Puilaurens)
Altitude	Between 335m and 850m
Total Ascent	10m (830m Camps-sur-l'Agly to Puilaurens)
Total Descent	520m (890m Camps-sur-l'Agly to Puilaurens)
IGN 1:25,000 Maps	2347OT (Quillan) and 2348ET (Prades)

Navigation
This link coincides for its whole length with the GR36 long-distance path, so you will see red and white waymarks.

As described below, there is a slightly tricky section near Malabrac, where the waymarks need to be followed carefully.

At la Couillade **(10)**, the trail divides – the North Variant turns right, the link goes left. Thereafter, take care, because the waymarking just after this fork was not very clear at the time of writing.

The link goes along the edge of the pasture ahead, then bears right to go through a gap in a fence. It begins to descend fairly abruptly, and quickly becomes a rough, brown-surfaced track, but the slope soon eases and the landscape begins to open out. You bear to the right, then cross a most beautiful open **plateau**, near the Col del Bedau.

The trail crosses this upland pastureland, and after a barely detectable rise in the ground, you meet, on the left, the end of a jeep track. Turn left onto the jeep track and follow it as it winds gently downhill. You are now crossing semi-open ground.

As the track descends to the south, take particular care to watch out for where the Sentier Cathare/GR36 forks off onto a grassy footpath to the left **(12)**. (The track itself bears right and soon comes to the near-deserted hamlet of Malabrac. If you find yourself there, turn back and search for the correct turning.)

The link crosses this lovely high, open plateau, near the Col de Bedau

At the time of writing, the 1:25,000 map is a little out of date just here, so follow the waymarked path cautiously. The trail descends, bears right, and becomes an earth track between rows of box trees. At a shady T-junction, turn left.

The trail crosses more semi-open ground, level again. You pass an old well on the right, then the path enters woodland, starting to descend not long afterwards.

The next section of the trail goes down an especially steep slope, zigzagging over bare rock and stretches of loose stones on the way. Take your time on this descent, and be particularly cautious when the ground is wet. En route, however, there are magnificent views down to Caudiès-de-Fenouillèdes and to the high ground beyond.

After two crossings of a small ravine, the slope eases a little. The descent continues, now in shaded, evergreen-oak woodland. You finally emerge onto relatively open ground, and eventually the path joins a lane on the edge of vineyard country.

Although the sign says 'No vehicles', walkers are welcome – in the background, the Pech de Bugarach

Follow the lane to meet the D9 and turn left, soon to approach Caudiès **(3)**. Cross a handsome bridge over the

Boulzane river, enter the town, and continue up the road beyond the bridge.

At the top of the slope the Sentier Cathare is way-marked to continue straight ahead, but you may prefer to turn right to follow the broad street that leads into the centre of Caudiès. There, turn right into the square, then bear left and quickly emerge onto the main D117. Turn left and go along the D117 for a short distance to a crossing by a corner shop. Here you rejoin the Main Route.

Notes for west–east walkers
Take special care on a complicated section from the T-junction of tracks, just east of Malabrac, as far as the plateau near the Col del Bedau.

POINTS OF INTEREST

Plateau Near the Col del Bedau This vast, open space commands very extensive views. The south face of the Pech de Bugarach looms up not far to the north, and the Fenouillèdes Hills, backed by Canigou mountain, stretch far to the south – it is a wonderful landscape.

The track you are following here is also of interest. It is described in a local walks guidebook as the *chemin du facteur*, a path formerly taken by the postman when delivering mail to remote hamlets and farmsteads, which are today mostly deserted and ruined. Apparently, the postman's main occupational hazard was that he would return home in the evening with a thick head, having been pressed at each settlement to take a glass of something alcoholic 'to help him on his way'.

STAGE 6 (MAIN ROUTE)
Puilaurens to Quirbajou (or Labeau)

The highlight of today's trek is the fearsome fortress of Puilaurens, a well-known Cathar castle that is reached soon after starting out.

This stage is also another demanding one. Forests dominate most of the landscape, and the longest climb comes right at the end, up the north slope of the remote Rébenty Valley.

After Puilaurens Castle, the trail proceeds to Axat, in the upper Aude Valley. This is a good place to stock up and seek refreshment.

Accommodation beyond Axat is limited. There is a *gîte d'étape* in Quirbajou, as well as at Labeau (7), close to a horse-riders' alternative route west of Marsa.

If you want to travel from Axat to Quillan, see 'Planning a Trek' in the introduction.

Distance	23.5km to Quirbajou and to Labeau
Walking time	6 hours to Quirbajou; 5 hours 45 mins to Labeau (allow also at least 1 hour to walk up to Puilaurens Castle, tour the fortress and return to the trail)
Altitude	Between 400m and 810m to Quirbajou; between 400m and 660m to Labeau
Total Ascent	670m to Quirbajou; 520m to Labeau (in addition, there is a climb of about 150m from the trail to Puilaurens Castle)
Total Descent	320m
IGN 1:25,000 Maps	2348ET (Prades) and 2248ET (Axat/Quérigut); Puilaurens is in map fold 1B of the Prades map; on the Axat/Quérigut map, Quirbajou is in map fold 7A, Labeau is in map fold 6A.

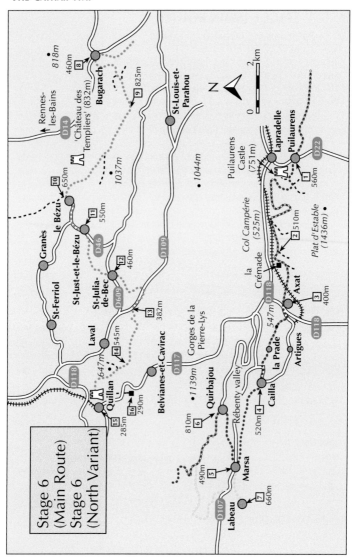

Stage 6 (Main Route)
Stage 6 (North Variant)

Navigation
At Marsa (5) the walkers' route, with blue and yellow waymarks, crosses the Rébenty river and climbs to Quirbajou, while the horse-riders' alternative route, waymarked orange, continues westwards up the valley to Labeau (7).

From the D22 in Puilaurens (1) the trail climbs through the village, bearing to the right. Follow the path signposted for the château. You soon enter a forest and start to ascend steeply. At the top, you emerge into an open area – this is a car park for visitors to **Puilaurens Castle**. A ticket office for the castle is on the right, and the castle is on a hill above that.

(If you start from Lapradelle, head south down the D22, back towards Puilaurens. Not long after leaving Lapradelle, you will see, on the right, a path climbing

Puilaurens Castle, high above Puilaurens village

into the forest and clearly signposted for Puilaurens Castle. Take this path and meet the trail by the ticket office. It takes hardly any longer to walk from Lapradelle to the ticket office than from Puilaurens.)

Returning to the ticket office after visiting the castle, walk along the castle's access road. You soon come to another open area – here turn sharp right off the access road onto a wide forest track.

Keep to this track through the forest for about 4km. At first it bears to the right and affords splendid views towards the eastern side of Puilaurens Castle, then turns sharp left and traverses a steep slope. In due course it bears to the left, then winds steeply downhill. After various twists and turns, it reaches the edge of an open area and goes left, but you head straight on across the open ground, towards a bridge over a railway line. This is the Col Campérie.

Just before you reach the bridge, turn left and follow a track that runs parallel to the railway line. This is the line from Rivesaltes, near Perpignan, to Axat. ◀ The track later bears left, away from the railway line. At the top of a slope, be careful to take a waymarked path going off to the right (**2**). This path descends through the forest and meets another track, where there is a small lake on the left.

Little red trains, full of tourists waving enthusiastically, run along here in summer – see 'Getting Around', in the introduction.

Turn left along this track, which passes (on the right) a large campsite (la Crémade). Continue straight ahead. Just after crossing a couple of small streams and approaching a big open area, turn right onto another track.

Shortly afterwards, in semi-open country, go left at a track fork. A little further along, the ground suddenly falls away, and you have a splendid view down into the Aude Valley. The trail zigzags down the hillside, crosses the railway line and enters **Axat (3)**. Descend steeply through the town's narrow streets and, just below a church, cross the River Aude by either of the two bridges (one very old, one more modern).

On the other side of the river, go left along the D118. Fork right, up a side road signposted for Artigues

that leads to a railway station, and at the station car park go right at another fork, still on the Artigues road. Follow that road as it swings right, crosses the railway by a bridge, then swings left. Almost immediately thereafter, leave the road, turning sharp right up a track that climbs above the town.

The track winds up the hillside, covered in scrub vegetation, then enters open farmland. Beyond a col at 547m you descend into a pretty valley, then lower down pass a large modern farm building, then, on your right, the centuries-old, but now partly crumbling hamlet of la Prade.

From here the trail forks right, down la Prade's narrow access lane. Further along, the lane climbs, then swings to the left around the spur of a hill. You are now on the upper slopes of the **Rébenty Valley**.

The lane descends and meets a tarmacked road. Turn left and go up the road, all the way to the hilltop village of Cailla **(4)**. Here, after barely entering the village, the Sentier Cathare goes sharp left, then almost immediately turns right down a lane. En route you pass Zig'ânes, the place from where donkeys can be hired for treks in the region.

Axat, where running the rapids is all the rage

109

Cailla – if you are beginning to feel the weight of your rucksack, you can hire a donkey here to carry it for you

The lane winds downhill, passing a barn and a farm before becoming an unsurfaced track and starting to climb. The trail enters a shady woodland and terraces uneventfully along the side of the valley for the next few kilometres. It finally joins a track and descends to the village of Marsa **(5)**.

From just beyond the church in Marsa the walkers' route of the trail crosses the River Rébenty by the nearby bridge. On the other side turn right, along the D107 through the village.

Near the edge of the village, fork left onto a grass track, skirt the river for a few metres, then go left again up a footpath that climbs the hillside. The path takes you on a long, demanding, but mostly shaded ascent to a high terrace. Here sits the village of Quirbajou **(6)**.

The El Cadet *gîte d'étape* is at the eastern end of the village, on the right.

Alternative Route from Marsa to Labeau

From near the bridge over the river in Marsa **(5)**, an alternative route for horse riders is indicated by orange

The gîte d'étape *in Quirbajou*

waymarks. It does not cross the River Rébenty but continues west, along a track on the southern bank of the river. After about 1km this route turns right and crosses a tributary stream at a ford.

A short distance beyond, you meet an unsurfaced track. If you turn left here, the track, which later becomes a steep, slightly overgrown footpath, takes you up to Labeau (**7**), although it is better to continue for a little distance, then turn left onto a tarmacked lane and follow that to Labeau instead. The lane is not waymarked, but the route to the *gîte d'étape* is obvious.

Notes for west–east walkers
From the track by a small lake beyond the la Crémade campsite, be sure to take the path on the right. On reaching another track at point (**2**) after a short climb, go left.

111

POINTS OF INTEREST

Puilaurens Castle After the Cathars lost the bastion of Montségur in 1244, Puilaurens was one of the places where the few surviving Bons Hommes and Bonnes Femmes sometimes took refuge, although this was not the case for long.

Today this fortress presents one of the most formidable appearances of all the castles passed on the Sentier Cathare. This appearance is the result of reconstruction work carried out after the Cathar period, when Puilaurens was rebuilt as a royal fortress to defend France's new southern frontier. It is one of the best preserved of the Cathar castles, and has been described as 'a model of medieval military architecture'. It also offers a superb viewpoint over the surrounding dramatic countryside.

The castle is open every day from April to October, and during weekends in February, March and November. It is closed in December and January (except in the Christmas holiday period).

Alongside the path that leads up to the castle from the ticket office are several shrubs and trees typical of the region. Signs give their names in French, including *bruyère* – heather, *buis* – box, *cerisier* – cherry tree, *chêne pubescent* – white oak, *chêne vert* – holm oak, *églantier* – wild rose, *épine noire* – blackthorn, *genévrier* – juniper, and *pin sylvestre* – Scots pine.

Axat This town is stretched out on the banks of the wide, fast-flowing River Aude, where rafting and canoeing are popular. The railway line crosses the valley on a high, horseshoe-shaped viaduct.

Rébenty Valley The River Rébenty has carved a long, deep trench running almost due west–east through the landscape. The valley has some charming villages, such as Marsa, with a renowned Romanesque church, but its remoteness is its chief feature. Vast forests cover most of its slopes, and bears pass through them from time to time. In fact in 2004 a bear emerged from the woods near Niort, higher up the valley, and polished off a couple of pigs for breakfast. It was eventually chased away, although it was clearly reluctant to depart.

STAGE 6 (NORTH VARIANT)
Bugarach to Quillan

The Cathars had a strong following in the country crossed by this long, hilly stage of the trail, although there are only a couple of hints of their existence in today's landscape. The Château des Templiers, on a ridge east of le Bézu, apparently had more to do with the Cathars than the Templars, and Rennes-le-Château, visible from the trail near le Bézu, is famous for unproven legends about Cathar treasure discovered by Saunière, the parish priest (and, as almost everyone knows, key characters in Dan Brown's *The Da Vinci Code* had the names Bézu Fache and Jacques Saunière).

Near the end of this stage, you are greeted with sudden and splendid views of Quillan and the Aude Valley.

See the sketch map accompanying Stage 6 (Main Route).

Distance	23.5km
Walking time	6 hours 15 mins
Altitude	Between 290m and 825m
Ascent/Descent	700m/880m
IGN 1:25,000 Map	2347OT (Quillan); Bugarach is in map fold 8C, Quillan is in map fold 3C

Navigation
The *gîte d'étape* at the outdoor centre called la Forge, just south of Quillan, can be reached by following a horse-riders' alternative route, which is indicated by orange waymarks.

From the D14 just below Bugarach **(8)**, go southwest down a winding tarmacked lane signposted for the Maison de Nature et Randonnée. Where the lane swings left the second time, go straight on, up a possibly muddy track. It climbs steadily, bears to the right and enters

Landscape near the start of Stage 6 (North Variant)

woodland. A little further along, turn sharp left off the track onto a path leading into a pine forest.

The path climbs steeply, then turns sharp right, where it becomes a track. The track winds uphill and meets a forest track. Turn right along that track and follow it for some distance, as it climbs steadily through the forest.

You finally reach the Col du Vent **(9)**, from where you may be able to see Canigou mountain, standing out on the horizon to the south.

Take the first track on the right and start a long descent through the forest of St-Just-et-le-Bézu. From time to time the view opens out to the north, where there is a wonderful panorama that can extend as far as the Montagne Noire, north of Carcassonne. Closer, also to the north, is a rocky, serrated ridge on which, although hardly visible from the trail, is the **Château des Templiers**, also known as the Château du Bézu.

After crossing a cattle-grid you come to a track fork where you go right. Soon the forest is replaced, first by semi-open ground, then by pastureland on either side. Cross another cattle-grid and pass to the right of a big barn. The slope levels out and a new vista opens up to the left. From near here you may be able to see a large, whitish tower on a hill about 20km to the west. That is Puivert Castle, near the end of Stage 7 of the Sentier Cathare.

Where a track goes off on the left down a valley towards the hamlet of le Bézu, resist the temptation to follow it, and continue straight on towards a col **(10)** lying above and to the right of le Bézu. ▶

At the col turn left, passing a small cemetery on the right, and descend towards le Bézu. You pass a church on the right, then swing to the left. Follow what is by now a tarmacked road, as it describes a loop and passes just below the hamlet.

Continue down this road, which descends to the bottom of a valley and then climbs up the other side. When you meet the D46, turn left. Pass a stone cross on the right, and a little further along, just after crossing a stream,

From the col you may be able to see, on a hilltop to the north, Rennes-le-Château.

Stage 6 of the North Variant starts in Bugarach village and traverses the high slopes on the left

Looking west from near le Bézu

turn left off the road onto a footpath that has box trees on both sides. The path soon meets a track, where you turn left. This track in turn brings you down to the D46 again, just outside the hamlet of St-Just-et-le-Bézu **(11)**.

Keep to the road as it goes through the hamlet, then, with a washplace on the left, turn onto a lane on the right that passes into open country. Pass a stone cross on the right, and shortly afterwards the lane enters woodland and starts to descend. It narrows and becomes a stony path, and after emerging into open country again, drops into the valley on the left and crosses a small stream at a ford.

The path beyond curves to the left and drops down to a road. Turn left onto the road, which passes a former mill on the right. The trail then embarks upon a long climb to the pretty hamlet of St-Julia-de-Bec **(12)**, which has street names in the Occitan language. There, you pass a fine fountain, then bear to the left and climb out of the hamlet.

At the far end of the hamlet you pass, on the left, a small washplace below ground level, then bear to the right and pick up a jeep track heading south. Where the track forks by a metal cross, go right. You come down to a tarmacked lane and turn left along that. Just before the lane bears right towards a group of buildings, go left, down an unsurfaced track. This descends towards the valley ahead.

The track executes a hairpin bend to the left (although you can cut off this bend with an obvious path going past a ruined stone building), then joins another track that approaches from the right. Cross a river by a solid-looking bridge, then follow the track, first alongside the river, then uphill into the woods on the other side of the valley.

Emerging onto the D109, turn right and walk down the road for about 15 minutes. Just after the road crosses a bridge and starts to swing right, turn left onto a jeep track going into a forest (13). The track immediately forks, and here you turn left. The track winds steeply up the slope ahead.

Eventually the slope eases a little and you begin a long westward traverse along the north slope of a ridge. Towards the end of this traverse, you pass the Col des Trois Quilles (14) on the left. From the Col des Trois Quilles there is a marvellous view down into the deep, wide valley of the River Aude. The northern end of the narrow, steep-sided Gorges de la Pierre-Lys is visible on the left.

A little further on, at another col, the track swings to the right and two signposted paths go off to the left. Be careful to take the first of those (the second goes up to the summit of the hill directly ahead, Bitrague, 647m).

Cross to the other side of the ridge and Quillan immediately comes into view ahead. On reaching another col, cross back to the other side of the ridge and follow a path, now in pine forest. In due course this path descends to a track, where you go right. Pass beneath a power line, and the track becomes a path that winds downhill towards Quillan.

Eventually you emerge onto a tarmacked road on a new housing estate. Follow the road downhill for a short distance, then, where that road bears to the right, continue straight on, along a lane with a 'No Through Road' sign. This soon brings you to a corner of the medieval castle that overlooks Quillan (the castle can be entered on the left).

Descend to the right of the castle, bear left, then turn sharp right to go down a steep, narrow street, bringing you out on a road in Quillan just opposite the old bridge over the River Aude. The market place and centre of **Quillan (15)** are on the other side of the bridge.

Alternative If you want to go to la Forge **(16)**, turn left, alongside the river, to approach the Formica factory (now closed). Follow the orange waymarks down the road going straight ahead. At first there are factory buildings on both sides, and later, on the outskirts of Quillan, cross an open space on the right. Reach and cross a green metal bridge that spans the River Aude – la Forge is on the left, on the other side of the main road.

Notes for west–east walkers

Almost immediately after the start of this stage, you follow a route that is different from that shown in edition 2 of the IGN 1:25,000 Quillan map. As you climb out of Quillan, be sure to follow the waymarks that lead you below and to the left of the castle.

On reaching the col above le Bézu **(10)**, take the first track on the right. A track coming up on the right from le Bézu soon joins your track, and shortly after that you may see a sign saying 'Propriété Privée'. That can be ignored. Soon after that, also ignore jeep tracks going off to the left – carry straight on towards the forest and limestone cliffs ahead.

At the Col du Vent **(9)**, take the first track on the left. From here you start the long descent towards Bugarach. Then, not long after passing under a small power line, be careful to take a well-waymarked left turn onto a smaller track descending into the forest.

POINTS OF INTEREST

Château des Templiers The Templars were a medieval military–religious order which, like the Cathars, also came to grief. The helpful website www.languedoc-france.info says, 'In the popular imagination (and books about Rennes-le-Château) this is an old Templar fortress, from where the Templars' treasure was rescued when they were persecuted by the French king...There is very little evidence that it was ever a Templar fortress, but plenty that it was a Cathar stronghold... It is known that Cathar bishops took refuge here. It appears that the château was never besieged, but it surrendered without a fight (to the French) after the demoralising fall of the château of Termes in 1210.'

Quillan This large country town is a base for tourism in Cathar castle country and the Pyrenees, and for rafting and other adventure sports in the Aude Valley. The bulky, square-shaped medieval castle on the town's eastern slope was a stronghold of the Cathars' opponents.

In the centre of Quillan, looking back to the castle

STAGE 7 (MAIN ROUTE)
Quirbajou (or Labeau) to Puivert

Near the end of this stage you can tick off another Cathar castle – the fortress of Puivert. Bigger, better preserved, but less awesome in appearance than most Cathar castles, Puivert was a centre of Occitan music and culture before being seized by the French invaders.

If you start from Labeau (1), this is a long and strenuous stage of the trail, with, in particular, a big climb out of the Rébenty Valley. From Quirbajou (4) you face a stage of average length and severity.

Much of this stage, especially the first half, passes through forest. The trees block any extensive views, but it is a fine forest with some splendid tree specimens, and if you keep your eyes open and minimise the noise you make, you may see deer or wild boar.

Karst features, such as enclosed basins and *avens* (vertical chasms in the rock), have been formed in the limestone of this area.

Distance	22.5km from Quirbajou; 27.5km from Labeau
Walking time	5hours 45 mins from Quirbajou; 7 hours 15 mins from Labeau (in addition, allow an hour to visit Puivert Castle, which is immediately next to the trail)
Altitude	Between 485m and 1150m
Total Ascent	480m from Quirbajou; 800m from Labeau
Total Descent	810m from Quirbajou; 970m from Labeau
IGN 1:25,000 Maps	2248ET (Axat/Quérigut), 2347OT (Quillan) and 2247OT (Lavelanet); on the Axat/Quérigut map, Quirbajou is in map fold 7A, Labeau is in map fold 6A; Puivert is in map fold 8C of the Lavelanet map

Navigation
If you start at Labeau (1) on the horse-riders' alternative route, follow orange waymarks to point (3). There you join the walkers' route, which carries blue and yellow waymarks.

From just south of Nébias **(8)** to Puivert Castle the route of the Sentier Cathare and that of the GR7 long-distance path coincide. There are therefore red and white waymarks on this section of the trail.

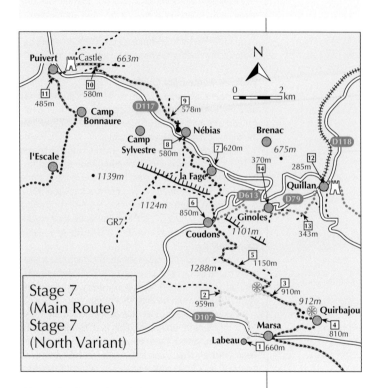

Puivert Castle 663m
[11] 485m
[10] 580m
Camp Bonnaure
D117
[9] 578m
l'Escale
Camp Sylvestre
[8] 580m
Nébias
Brenac
675m
• 1139m
la Fage
370m
[14]
[12] 285m
Quillan
1124m
[6] 850m
D613
D79
GR7
Ginoles
[13] 343m
Coudons
1101m
• 1288m
[5] 1150m
Stage 7 (Main Route)
Stage 7 (North Variant)
[2] 959m
[3] 910m
912m
Quirbajou
D107
Marsa
[4] 810m
Labeau
[1] 660m
N
0   2 km
D118

Alternative Route from Labeau to (3)

The alternative route from Labeau **(1)** descends into the Rébenty Valley, picks up orange waymarks and crosses the River Rébenty by a bridge.

Turn left along the D107 and go along it for a very short distance, before forking right onto a path going up into the wooded hillside. There is a hard climb ahead, and although the path is wide, it can be wet in places. At first the slope is relatively moderate, but higher up it becomes steep. After a final stiff haul, you reach a well-made track at point **(2)**.

Turn right along the track. This is a splendid balcony route with extensive views, especially to the west, towards the Plateau de Sault and the high hills and mountains beyond. Eventually you reach the walkers' route of the Sentier Cathare **(3)**. Here, turn sharp left.

Walkers' Route from Quirbajou

The Sentier Cathare heads due west out of Quirbajou **(4)** on a well-made track that passes to the south of a hill called Pujol de Sougranet (912m). En route you pass, on the right, an *aven* covered by a grille.

The track, now in semi-open grazing land that seems to be especially favoured by multi-coloured butterflies, bears to the left as it is joined by another track coming from Quirbajou. Eventually you reach a track fork **(3)** – go right here. (**Note** If you take the left fork for a short distance, then scramble up a low limestone wall on the right, you will see another *aven* – a sizeable one – also covered by a grille.)

A long, steady climb lies ahead. The track you are on bears round to the right, then, in a patch of open ground, the trail veers to the left, and shortly afterwards forks left again. By now you have entered a forest.

The trail passes over a col and descends a short distance into a more open area. This is in fact an entirely closed basin, caused by solution of the underlying limestone. After another climb and another col **(5)**, you start what will be a long, almost unbroken descent extending for many kilometres.

In due course you come to a T-junction of tracks, where you turn right. After a short climb, you go over the Col de Camelier. Now on a wide forest track, zigzag downhill and finally emerge into open country and reach the village of Coudons **(6)**.

Turn right and walk along the D613 (the village is on the left). You soon meet the North Variant of the trail, from Quillan, where it emerges from the forest on the right. Carry straight on, along the road, away from Coudons.

Where the road swings to the right, turn left onto a tarmacked lane. This takes you past a large wooden barn, on the left. Where the lane swings left towards a house, continue straight on, along a jeep track. You are now crossing semi-open farmland. At a track fork, bear right.

In due course, take a left turn and pass under a power line. In woodland again, the path soon starts to descend more steeply, zigzagging down the slope. You meet a forest track that you go straight across. Where the slope becomes gentler, the path emerges into open country.

Approach the hamlet of la Fage **(7)** and skirt the western side of this settlement. Turn left onto a track heading west, out of the hamlet. This track terraces below cliffs high up on the left. A wide, almost flat expanse of farmland (part of a **former lake**) is below on the right.

In due course, after passing through a stretch of woodland, take a right turn at a track junction to go

Fountain in Nébias marking the Atlantic/ Mediterranean watershed

downhill along the edge of a field. At a track crossing at the bottom of the field, turn left. Nébias is now not far away on the right, and you may be able to see Puivert Castle on a hill a few kilometres away in the distance ahead. Further on, at yet another crossing, go right.

When you reach the D117, cross carefully and enter **Nébias (8)**. Go to the left of the church and the town square to reach a T-junction (the museum in Nébias is almost directly opposite). Turn left down what is the principal east–west street through the village. On the edge of the village, fork right down the Allée de la Chapelle. Pass to the right of the Ste-Claire chapel, and you are then on a track taking you out into open country.

The lane eventually brings you to a track junction where there are several footpath signposts **(9)**. Carry straight on here (that is, take the left-most track).

Continue towards and through the wooded area ahead. There follows a long stretch which at first is almost on the level, and later becomes a path traversing up the slope ahead. There are various crossings and forks, but the trail, usually straight ahead, is well indicated. The path eventually emerges onto a track where you turn right **(10)**.

After a further steady climb, you meet another track, running along the ridge of the hill. Turn left there to descend gently and approach the entrance to **Puivert Castle**, directly ahead.

After visiting the castle, pick up the trail again as it passes beneath the southern walls of the fortress. At the far end of a car park the GR7 turns right, along a track, while the Sentier Cathare goes down a footpath on the left. This descends steeply and, as it does so, you catch glimpses of Puivert, below on the right.

Eventually the path reaches a large chapel. The trail passes in front of this building, then emerges just beyond a bend on the D117. Take great care here. Turn right and follow the road for a short distance, then turn sharp left down a minor road. At a road junction below, turn sharp right into **Puivert (11)**. You pass Puivert's museum, on the right, and then come to a splendid, covered market hall.

Notes for west–east walkers
Please take careful account of the advice given in the introduction to this stage.

Looking down on Puivert village from the western end of the castle, where remains of the Cathars' fortress have been located

POINTS OF INTEREST

Puivert Castle Before the crusade against the Cathars, this castle was a renowned centre of Occitan culture, where troubadours and poets received a generous welcome, but the castle fell to the French army in 1210, after only three days of assault. Legend has it that the Cathar lord of Puivert escaped from the castle by a secret underground tunnel, with his young son in his arms, only seconds before French soldiers burst into the room where they had taken refuge.

The east front of Puivert Castle, as seen from the trail

Most of the castle as we see it today was in fact constructed by a wealthy French family in the 14th century – well after the period in which Cathars lived here. Remains of the Cathar fortress are at the far western end. Perhaps because it never presented any serious military threat to anyone, it was never systematically demolished. It suffered from neglect and pillage after the Revolution, but some restoration has been carried out more recently.

The interior of the castle is particularly well known for its sculptures of musicians with their instruments, which invoke the castle's pre-crusade fame as a centre for music and culture. Re-created medieval instruments are in the Salle de Musiciens. The castle is open all year.

Former Lake The large expanse of almost flat land stretching to the south of Nébias and Puivert was formerly occupied by a lake. It covered nearly 200 hectares and was about 15m deep, but in the late 13th century the barrier holding back the lake, at Puivert, suddenly burst and the water drained away, causing enormous damage in the valley downriver. Mirepoix was completely destroyed. Whether the catastrophe was the result of natural causes, or the lake was deliberately drained, perhaps so that the land could be used for agriculture, remains unclear.

Nébias Nébias has a small wildlife museum, open most afternoons from April to October inclusive. A fountain by the museum tells you that you are about to cross the continental watershed – streams to the east flow towards the Mediterranean, those to the west head for the Atlantic.

The remains of a stone-built windmill sit on a hill to the north of the village, and the limestone plateau beyond has been eroded in a most entertaining way. The rock has been carved into deep channels and depressions, which all link up to make an intricate labyrinth. This fascinating stretch of karst landscape is well worth exploring if you have the time.

The tiny, recently restored Ste-Claire Chapel on the Sentier Cathare just west of Nébias is possibly the smallest chapel on the trail. It was originally built in 1600 on the site of an older oratory, where there was said to be a miraculous spring whose water could cure eye diseases.

Puivert This attractive little settlement is wedged into a gap in the ridge on which the castle is located. Local history and medieval musical instruments are the subjects of displays in the museum in the village (the Musée du Quercorb), which is open from April to early November.

STAGE 7 (NORTH VARIANT)
Quillan to Puivert

The route of this stage of the North Variant between Coudons **(6)** and Puivert **(11)** is as for Stage 7 (Main Route).

This is quite a strenuous stage. The delightful countryside between Quillan **(12)** and Ginoles **(14)** is open, spacious and surrounded by hills and cliffs, but then you face an especially long, steady climb out of the Aude Valley up to Coudons **(6)**.

See the sketch map accompanying Stage 7 (Main Route).

Distance	20.5km
Walking time	5 hours 45 mins.
Altitude	Between 285m and 850m.
Ascent/Descent	700m/500m
IGN 1:25,000 Maps	2347OT (Quillan) and 2247OT (Lavelanet); Quillan is in map fold 3C of its map, Puivert is in map fold 8C of the Lavelanet map

Navigation
Please read the introduction to Stage 7 (Main Route).

If you stayed overnight at the *gîte d'étape* at la Forge, return by the previous day's route towards the centre of Quillan. Cross the River Aude by a bridge near the entrance to the Formica factory, turn left near the post office, then turn right and follow the main road towards some traffic lights.

From the traffic lights in the centre of Quillan **(12)**, on the main road through the town, follow the D79, going west in the direction signposted for Ginoles. Cross

the railway line. A horse-riders' alternative route, via Brenac, is signposted up a road on the right (it rejoins the walkers' route at Nébias), but you should follow the D79 round to the left.

Where the D79 turns off to the right, carry straight on along a minor road. Later, turn right along the Chemin de Castillou. This passes between houses and winds up the slope ahead. The slope soon levels out, and you are then on a stony track in open country

After a little while you come to a fork in the track (**13**) where you go right. A little further along, the track starts to descend. ▶ At the bottom of the hill, and immediately before the track fords a stream, turn left and go along the edge of a field. Turn right over an old stone bridge, then follow the path ahead. At a junction with a stony track, turn left along that track. This brings you down to a minor road, where you turn left and follow the road, with Ginoles immediately above on your right. Where the road bends left, take a sharp turn to the right, cross a stream, then climb a steep lane into the village (**14**).

Scene in Quillan; Stage 7 of the North Variant climbs and crosses the hills in the background.

There is an old photograph on a board showing that today's delightful view from this point towards the village of Ginoles is very similar to the view from here of a century ago.

Ginoles

Just after entering the village, turn left up a narrow street. At the top, turn right. Bear left just before the D79, and pass a church on the left and a cemetery on the right. After a short while you leave the village and approach a large metal cross with a covered reservoir on the right. Here go right, up a rough track.

The track swings left, then starts a steep climb up the shoulder of the hill ahead. At first the terrain is bare and open, then you climb into a forest.

In due course the trail swings right to cross a valley. There are wonderful views to Quillan, the Trois Quilles ridge, which you crossed on Stage 6, and to the right, huge cliffs which hang above Ginoles. The path swings left and there is then a steep uphill section where the

ground consists mainly of bare rock. (There is an unway-marked path on the right. It regains the main path later on, after a longer but less steep ascent of this section.)

You soon come up to a wide, well-made forest track where you go right. This comes into an open area and starts to swing to the right. Here you take a path climbing back into the forest on the left. This path through the forest eventually levels out and joins the D613 at a point **(6)** where you can see Coudons immediately on your left. Here, turn right along the D613.

You are now back on the Main Route of the trail. Follow this all the way to Puivert – see the route description for Stage 7 (Main Route).

Quillan and the Aude valley from Stage 7 of the North variant. Stage 6 approached the town from over the hills in the distance.

Notes for west–east walkers
Some careful route-finding is needed through Ginoles **(14)**, and across the country immediately after it.

If, at the end of this stage, you are heading for the *gîte d'étape* at la Forge, just south of Quillan, see the route description for Stage 6 (North Variant).

STAGE 8
Puivert to Espezel (or Belvis)

There are no castles on this stage of the trail, but a different kind of monument to resistance by local people to invasion by outside forces lies close to the trail. This is a restored forest cabin that served in the Second World War as the Poste de Commandement (PC) du Maquis – a base for Resistance fighters. In addition, a museum of peasant life in Espezel contains furniture, tools and other artefacts which, although only around a couple of hundred years old, are in many cases probably very similar to those made and employed by peasant farmers in this region in the 13th century, during the time of the Cathars.

This stage is untypical in a number of respects. For example, it runs along a north–south axis, not, as most other stages do, east–west. It is also unusual in that it crosses two wide areas of nearly flat farmland.

There are two terminuses at the southern end of this stage – the principal route goes to the village of Espezel, and an alternative goes to Belvis and the nearby *gîte d'étape* of La Gineste (**9**).

Distance	17km (for both southern terminuses)
Walking time	4 hours 30 mins (for both southern terminuses)
Altitude	Between 485m and either 930m (en route to Espezel) or 1020m (en route to Belvis)
Ascent/Descent	600m to Espezel, 690m to Belvis/190m to Espezel, 300m to Belvis
IGN 1:25,000 Map	2247OT (Lavelanet); Puivert is in map fold 8C, Espezel is in map fold 7D, Belvis and La Gineste are in map fold 9D

Navigation
The alternative Sentier Cathare route, between point (**4**) and Belvis/La Gineste (**9**), is not waymarked in blue and yellow. There are other waymarks along this alternative route, but they vary in colour and nature along the way. The route description, below, explains which waymarks help at certain points, and which are best ignored.

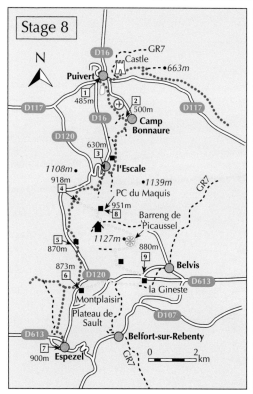

From the centre of Puivert (**1**) cross the river, and shortly after leaving the town come to a junction of minor roads. Take the left-most turning, along a tarmacked lane. This soon passes, on your right, a small lake. The trail then crosses a stream at a ford. On reaching a track/road junction, turn right, along an unsurfaced track.

You now cross a wide, flat expanse of land, with a landing strip used by gliders and light aircraft on the left. Puivert Castle sits on its hilltop, immediately behind you.

The track bears left, then follows a long, straight section towards the hamlet of Camp Bonnaure in the

Puivert village and castle

distance. On eventually reaching a crossing, go straight across and follow the track that rises to the left. Near the top of the rise, turn right, onto another track (**2**). You pass just below Camp Bonnaure, on the left.

The track descends, crosses a stream and rises again on the other side. After a little way, turn right onto another track. This soon bears to the left and descends to meet another stream. With the stream on the right, the track now goes up the valley ahead, with meadows on the left. It then crosses the stream, bears right and rises to meet a tarmacked lane. Turn left here.

Just after passing a building on the right, dated 1837, the lane ends and you walk straight ahead onto an unsurfaced track. As the track turns up into the hill, you enter woodland. At a fork in the track, turn sharp right and start to descend. The track winds downhill and eventually meets the stream again, where a local waymarked path goes off on the left, but you cross the stream, if necessary by a footbridge on the left.

Follow the track opposite uphill. It swings to the right, terraces along the side of the hill, then bears left and meets a tarmacked lane in the hamlet of **l'Escale (3)**. Turn left here. At a fork further along, go sharp right and climb steeply. At the top, the lane bears left. You pass to the left of both a memorial plaque and a church, then fork right towards a car park and leave l'Escale.

Further along the track, turn right onto a stony path, climbing steeply into the forest above. There is now a long ascent on this path as it zigzags up the hill. Eventually the slope eases, and you pass into a pine forest with mossy undergrowth.

Village church, l'Escale; in the bottom left-hand corner is a memorial recalling the deliberate destruction of the village in 1944

The trail eventually approaches an open area where logs may be stacked. Here, turn sharp left, then immediately sharp right. The trail bears to the left through a conifer plantation, climbing all the while.

At the top of the slope there is a path junction (**4**). Here, the main Sentier Cathare route, to Espezel, goes sharp right. The alternative route to Belvis/La Gineste turns off to the left (this is described below).

If you want to visit the **PC du Maquis**, but still end the day in Espezel, go down that alternative route for a little way, then return to this point.

Along the principal Sentier Cathare route beyond (**4**), take a left fork after a short distance. The next section of the route winds up and down through the forest and needs to be followed with particular care. The path goes through a clearing, then, after briefly re-entering woodland, meets another clearing. At the head of that second clearing, you turn to the left and climb steeply. When you come to a rough forest track, turn right. This track bears to the right and descends to emerge at the head of a well-made forest track – go straight ahead down that track.

Where the track eventually bears to the right, go left onto a footpath that contours around the side of the hill. The path descends to the right and meets another well-made forest track. Turn left and follow that track uphill for a short way. Just before it bears to the left, turn right onto another footpath, and drop steeply into the forest again.

You soon meet yet another well-made forest track, where you turn left – the track passes beneath some enormously tall and magnificent fir trees. It then bears to the right and descends towards open ground. Just on the right is a picnic spot near the ruin of a former forest cabin (**5**).

Cross the open ground ahead and reach the D120 – you are now on the Plateau de Sault. Cross the road and take a footpath that is very slightly on the right and which enters the forest opposite. At a junction reached after a short distance, turn left. You soon approach the road again, but do not go up to the road – instead, turn right and walk along a path that rises, then descends, following all the while the edge of an area of woodland.

Eventually you reach the far corner of the woodland, with conifers on the right. Cross the grass area ahead towards the buildings of Montplaisir **(6)**. You again approach the D120, but immediately turn right onto a well-made farm road that is heading almost due west.

After about 0.5km, turn left onto a track, signposted for Espezel, which heads south across the **Plateau de Sault**. After walking 2km along this track, follow it to the left. At the far end, turn right and pass through the little tunnel that goes under the D613. You then enter Espezel **(7)**.

Alternative Route to Belvis and La Gineste from (4)
At the path junction **(4)**, turn left – the path/track is waymarked by green arrows on a yellow background (although they are pointing back the way you have come). At an intersection of paths, go straight ahead, and after a short distance you reach, on the right, a stone cabin, the PC du Maquis **(8)**.

On its approach to Espezel, the Sentier Cathare follows this track across the near-flat Plateau de Sault

Follow the track heading downhill from the stone cabin across the open ground below. At the bottom, on the edge of the forest, turn left into the forest. After a short while fork right, onto a path that soon starts to wind steeply up the slope ahead. Eventually this path reaches a well-made forest track. Turn sharp right onto this track and follow it for a few metres up to a track crossing (opposite, there is an unlocked forest refuge – the Refuge du Maquis). Turn sharp left at the crossing and follow another well-made forest track, heading east.

The track terraces along the side of the hill, and there are fine views to the left, in the direction of Puivert. The track bends to the right and passes close to the awesome Barreng de Picaussel, a chasm nearly 100m deep. A few minutes later you reach a stunning viewpoint over the Pays de Sault (with Belvis on the left). Continuing along the track, you eventually approach a wide area for timber storage. Here, turn sharp left down a path with yellow waymarks.

The path winds down the hillside for some time, then meets a track at a bend in that track. Go straight ahead and follow this track. Pass to the right of a large white building (Fontblanche, also a *gîte*) and onto an access track just beyond. You are now on almost flat ground. The track bears to the left and eventually meets a minor road – **Belvis** is a little way up on the left. For La Gineste (**9**), turn right along the minor road to reach the D613 – the *gîte* is immediately opposite.

Notes for west–east walkers

On the main Sentier Cathare route, starting from Espezel, the trail, although well waymarked, needs to be followed with particular care through the forest between (**5**) and (**4**).

As noted earlier, the alternative route, from La Gineste/Belvis to (**4**), does not carry the usual blue and yellow Sentier Cathare waymarks. It is not a difficult route to follow, but as you progress along it, keep a careful note of your position on the 1:25,000 map.

POINTS OF INTEREST

L'Escale and the PC du Maquis L'Escale was burnt in August 1944 by Nazi troops in reprisal for its inhabitants having helped the French Resistance. The Resistance was known as the *'maquis'*, which means thorny scrub, very difficult to penetrate, and the *maquisards* were based in the hills nearby. Their base, the PC du Maquis, was a stone cabin **(8)**, and arms and explosives dropped by parachute by the British were used to harass the occupying forces. Just before setting l'Escale ablaze, the Nazis also destroyed the cabin, but the *maquisards* had already escaped and joined forces with another Resistance unit elsewhere in the mountains. The cabin was restored by former *maquisards* in 1993. It is always open, and there are panels explaining the history of the Resistance.

The Plateau de Sault A remarkably level and extensive basin of land which is almost completely enclosed by limestone hills. Occupied by a lake during the last ice age, this area is now rich farmland (the local farmers appear to be particularly proud of their potatoes).

Espezel Espezel has an excellent museum of local history, with many items from a peasant household of over a century ago. The treasures of this remarkable collection include a wardrobe carved entirely from the trunk of what must have been a giant fir tree, and an oil lamp almost identical to one recovered from the remains of the 13th-century Cathar village at Montségur. The museum is open until 6.00pm every day in July and August, and at other times by appointment.

Fountain in the centre of Espezel

Belvis A castle here, subsequently destroyed, sheltered Cathars fleeing from the Inquisition. The village has a museum of prehistory (but entry has to be pre-booked via the *mairie*), and traces of Neanderthal inhabitants were found in a cave nearby. They occupied it about 35,000 years ago, during the last ice age.

STAGE 9
Espezel (or Belvis) to Comus

Once again there are no Cathar castles to visit on this stage, although there are some great views. You have your first sight – a breathtaking one – of Montségur, the most famous of the Cathar castles, seen from the high, open ground of the splendid Plateau de Languerail. Later, you should also see in the distance the castle and village of Montaillou.

The final section, in forest, affords a tremendous view into the enormously deep Frau Gorge. Shortly afterwards you pass the highest point on the Sentier Cathare, the Col de la Gargante (**6**), at an altitude of 1352m.

Note Distance, walking time and so on are much the same, whether you start from Espezel or Belvis.

Distance	20km
Walking time	5 hours 15 mins
Altitude	Between 880m and 1350m
Ascent/Descent	500m/230m
IGN 1:25,000 Maps	2247OT (Lavelanet) and 2148ET (Ax-les-Thermes); on the Lavelanet map Espezel is in map fold 7D and Belvis and La Gineste are in map fold 9D, Comus is in map fold 9A of the Ax-les-Thermes map

Navigation
The alternative route from Belvis/La Gineste (**8**) to the point where it meets the principal route (**9**) is not indicated by Sentier Cathare waymarks. Part of the route carries the red and white waymarks of the GR7 long-distance path.

If you stayed overnight in Belvis or at La Gineste, please see the description below of the route from there to the principal route of the Sentier Cathare.

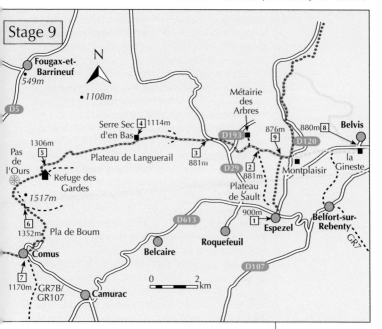

From Espezel (1) head north out of the village on a gravel lane and pass through the little tunnel that goes under the D613. After a short distance, turn left onto another track. Next is a long section across the Plateau de Sault.

Ignore a track that goes off to the right, and ditto one going left. It may then appear from the waymarking that the trail goes straight ahead, but you are advised instead to follow the main track as it swings to the right (i.e. retrace your footsteps of the previous day).

After more than 2km, reach a T-junction of tracks (9). You came in from the right yesterday, so turn left at this junction.

After about 1km along this well-made track, another track joins on the left (2). (The French guidebook to the trail describes a route from Espezel to this point that is different from the one just described, but at the time of writing (2005) that route is not well waymarked, is a little complicated to follow, and is hardly any shorter than the route suggested above.)

Carry straight on from **(2)**, and at the next junction go left, leaving the track on the right to go up to the Métairie des Arbres. After turning right at a track fork, then right again at a junction, you reach the D193. Cross the road and take the footpath opposite, which is fenced on both sides and weaves it way to the D29.

The Sentier Cathare follows a track on the other side of the D29, a very short distance on the right **(3)**. You at last leave the flat land behind and start to climb. After passing to the right of a small pylon, you enter woodland. The track climbs steadily, always on or close to the line of a ridge. Now and again there are fine views over the hills and forests to the left. At the various track forks, look out as usual for the trail's waymarks.

In due course the path chinks to the left and enters an open field – go right, along the edge of this open ground. You soon re-enter the forest on the right and continue in the same general direction. Then, after passing through a metal gate, descend to the ruins of the Serre Sec d'en Bas **(4)**.

The trail traverses the grass plateau ahead along a faintly defined track, bearing slightly to the left. After descending a little, it goes through a small wooden gate. You pass along the left-hand side of a fine line of beech trees, then cross into the meadow on the right and, still heading west, climb the slope ahead.

After passing through another small gate (a metal one) the trail climbs gently – once again alongside a line of superb beech trees. You are now on the **Plateau de Languerail**.

At the top of the rise, with a covered reservoir over on the right, Montségur Castle suddenly comes into view in the middle distance. In due course the trail starts to go downhill. Turn right on meeting the track at the bottom, then left just before reaching the edge of the open area at the top of the slope.

There follows a hard climb up a grass slope. Near the top, bear right. Here, you may well feel as if you are on top of the world.

At the end of the open area you cross a fence and enter woodland. The track eventually swings to the left and goes over a rocky hump. A few minutes later you emerge into a clearing with the Refuge des Gardes **(5)** on the left (the refuge is unlocked).

On the right is a forest road, onto which you turn. Later, just before the road swings to the left, you come to the Pas de l'Ours. From here there is a superb panorama over the Frau Gorge, plunging hundreds of metres below.

Follow the road round to the left, soon reaching the Col de la Gargante **(6)**. The trail continues along the forest road on the half-right.

The road contours around the hillside. It takes you out of the forest, and in due course there are views over the so-called Pla de Boum, below on the left. This huge, beautiful basin of pastureland is entirely enclosed, with no exit valley.

From the Sentier Cathare, high up on the Plateau de Languerail, walkers have their first view of Montségur Castle, on the steep-sided, isolated hill in the middle distance

143

The highest viewpoint on the trail – from the Pas de l'Ours down into the Frau Gorge and across to Montségur Castle

The road bears round to the right and reaches the Col du Boum, where a whole new landscape suddenly opens out. Continue along the road as it starts to descend gently. The church in Comus soon comes into view, below on the right, and far over on the left you may see **Montaillou**.

Take a footpath forking off the road to the right. It descends the grassy slope towards Comus, cutting off a bend in the road as it does so. The path becomes a grass track and winds down to **Comus (7)**. The trail goes straight down the road on the left, where you will find the *gîte d'étape*.

(If you are staying overnight at Camurac, follow the D20 southeast from Comus for 3km.)

Shepherd and flock, above Comus; the mountain in the background on the right is the Pic de Soularac, in the St-Barthélemy range

Alternative Route from Belvis/La Gineste to the Principal Route

From Belvis, return along the minor road by which you entered the village yesterday. Cross the D613 and reach the *gîte* of La Gineste (**8**). From here, follow the track that runs alongside the *gîte*. Keep on the track to where it crosses a stream, ignoring other tracks going off to nearby houses. Just beyond the stream you come to a track junction, where you turn right – you are now following the GR7.

After passing close to woodland on the left for some distance, you reach a track crossing. The GR7 turns left here, but you should turn right. After a short distance you reach the D613. Turn left and follow this road for about 200m, then fork right to follow the old route of the road, just before today's road bends to the left.

Where the old road itself bends to the left, carry straight on, along a well-made farm track. The track descends and eventually reaches the buildings of Montplaisir. Cross the D120 here and pick up another track, which heads in the same westward direction. After 0.5km, at a T-junction (**9**), you join the main route, coming in on the left. Carry straight on.

Notes for west–east walkers

Beyond the Pas de l'Ours, don't miss, on the left, the clearing where the Refuge des Gardes (**5**) is situated. Go over to the refuge, then take the track that heads off into the forest just to the left of the refuge.

The trail across the Plateau de Languerail, right down to the D29 (**3**), always lies on or not far from the west–east ridgeline, but there are many turns and forks on the path, and these need to be negotiated with care.

POINTS OF INTEREST

Plateau de Languerail This is the highest, and possibly the finest, of the several high plateaux that the Sentier Cathare traverses in its journey from the coast to Foix. There are views from here south towards the eastern Pyrenees, west to the high, bulky plateau of the Montagne de la Frau, and north towards the distant Montagne Noire region. Above all, there is a striking view of the limestone pinnacle on which is perched Montségur Castle. Coming from the east, this is the first view you have of Montségur, and it will probably stay with you as one of the outstanding images of your trek. Beyond Montségur, the crag on which stands Roquefixade Castle (end of Stage 11) is also visible in clear weather.

Montaillou The scant remains of Montaillou's former castle are on an open hill to the right of the village. Montaillou was a Cathar village *par excellence*, and its life around 1300 was documented in minute detail in the records of the Inquisition.

Comus Around this village the landscape is almost Alpine in appearance. There are hay meadows surrounding the village, pine forests on the nearby hills, and beyond, to the west, the high, jagged, often snow-covered Pic de Soularac. The *gîte d'étape* is renowned for the excellent food provided by its manager, Anne Pagès. The name of the friendly dog who resides at the gîte is Alf.

STAGE 10
Comus to Montségur

This stage finally brings you to Montségur, which will be the highlight of the trek for many people. Although it contains one long climb, it is a short stage, and you should reach Montségur by early afternoon, so might like to visit the castle, towering above the village, on this day.

This stage also passes through the spectacular Frau Gorge.

Distance	14.5km.
Walking time	3 hours 30 mins
Altitude	Between 605m and 1170m
Ascent/Descent	500m/750m
IGN 1:25,000 Maps	2148ET (Ax-les-Thermes) and 2247OT (Lavelanet); Comus is in map fold 9A of the Ax-les-Thermes map, Montségur is in map fold 2C of the Lavelanet map

Navigation
The Frau Gorge may be difficult to pass through during and just after periods of heavy rainfall. The main danger is from falling stones and rocks, and the path may also be partly washed away.

The eastern half of this stage is in Aude and the western half in Ariège. As noted earlier, blue and yellow waymarks are used for the Sentier Cathare in Aude, but not in Ariège.

The whole of this stage of the Sentier Cathare is also shared with two long-distance paths, the GR7B and the GR107 (the Chemin des Bonshommes). These trails carry red and white waymarks, and these are the waymarks to follow in Ariège (between leaving the Frau Gorge and Montségur).

From the lowest point of Comus (1), just beyond a war memorial, turn right to follow a narrow tarmacked lane that descends gently. You may see the limestone crown of the Montagne de la Frau directly ahead, gleaming in the morning sun.

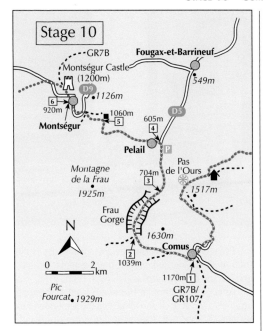

The lane soon becomes an unsurfaced forest road, and the valley sides and a forest begin to close in. A stream (the River Hers) runs alongside the track, on the left. At a fork in the forest road, go right.

Stay on that road for some distance until it bends sharply to the left **(2)**. Here, just beyond a notice that warns you of the danger of rockfalls in bad weather, go straight ahead onto a stony path that enters the **Frau Gorge**. This gorge is steep and wild, tightly enclosed at first by the valley walls and the forest on both sides. Later, you pass beneath gigantic rock faces, which rise directly from the valley bottom.

The trail continues to descend steeply, then you suddenly emerge onto a tarmacked road (the D5) **(3)**. Walk along that road as you continue down the valley – by now the downhill slope has eased considerably.

Travellers with a donkey set off from Comus

Eventually you pass, on the right, a picnic site by the river. At a road intersection just after the picnic site **(4)**, turn left and head towards and through Pelail.

After passing through this small hamlet, the road becomes a forest track and climbs up the semi-open valley ahead. Soon you fork right and enter woodland, where the trail becomes a path running alongside a stream on the left.

The path climbs steadily for some while, then crosses to the other side of the stream to immediately begin a much steeper ascent. It bears to the left, away from the stream, and at first zigzags up the slope. Later you meet, and for a short distance follow, a forest track. This becomes a path that climbs a rocky section on relatively open ground. There is a further steep section in the forest, then finally you reach the top of the climb. Here, the trail bears to the right.

After terracing for a while, the trail turns distinctly to the left **(5)** – the ruins of an old stone building are among trees on the right. For some distance ahead you now descend gradually, following what may be an ancient track bounded by the remains of stone walls and a line of trees. There is a deep, open valley on the right, and you may catch glimpses ahead of **Montségur Castle** on its high pinnacle.

In due course the trail swings to the right. It emerges into the open country and joins a lane, where you turn left. After a short distance turn right, off the lane, to take a path that descends into woodland below. (**Note** In the next section, ignore any home-made blue and yellow waymarks.)

The path zigzags down the steep slope, finally meeting a lane by a stream. Turn right and go over a bridge, then watch out for, on the left, a path going up into woodland (this path is not waymarked but it is well used). Take that cut-off path which, after a short distance, meets the D9. Cross the road, but take great care in doing so, as there is a blind curve on the right.

Fork right immediately onto a grass track opposite – you now cross an open area of meadows and vegetable plots just below **Montségur**, which is not far away on the right. The trail turns right at a track junction, and soon emerges into a large car park. Turn right and walk towards the far end of the car park.

Immediately after reaching the road beyond the car park, take the waymarked track that goes down on the right. After a very short distance, turn left onto a footpath that passes alongside more vegetable plots, just below Montségur. It passes between tall cypress hedges and enters the lower part of the village (**6**).

Notes for west–east walkers

The Sentier Cathare is waymarked to leave the lower part of Montségur (**6**) under a wide archway, then along a footpath which goes between two large cypress hedges. Be careful to follow red and white waymarks out of Montségur, and ignore any red and yellow ones.

In wet weather, the descent on a steep path through the forest to Pelail could be very slippery in places – take care.

Brace yourself for the ascent of the **Frau Gorge** – it is one of the steepest climbs on the trail.

Montségur Castle, right, high on its pinnacle above Montségur village

POINTS OF INTEREST

Montségur Castle, Village and Museum On the site of the castle remains there is evidence of human occupation that dates back to prehistoric times. There was some sort of fortified settlement here before the early 13th century, but very little is known about it. At the Cathars' request, and from around 1204, the settlement was rebuilt and its fortifications substantially strengthened. It became a Cathar stronghold – as a village, a religious centre and a fortress – and as many as 500 people may have been living there.

At the end of the siege of Montségur in 1244, over 200 Cathars were burnt at the stake just below the castle. There is a memorial to them on the path that leads to the castle (see also Conclusion, later in this book).

The Cathars' fortress was torn down and completely rebuilt, the new castle being occupied by a French garrison during subsequent centuries. But that fortification in turn was eventually abandoned and fell into its current semi-ruined state.

Nevertheless, Montségur Castle, on its limestone hill, is today the most powerful and probably the best known of all the images that are associated with the Cathars and Cathar castle country. It is also a memorable experience (and for many people a moving one) to scale the hill that the Cathars defended so tenaciously, and to look down from the castle as members of that besieged community did, knowing that they were staring at their place of execution. The castle is open all year, except in January.

After the siege the Cathar settlement there was destroyed, although a new settlement developed lower down, at the village's present location, eventually growing to its present size. There is very little traffic in the village, which is a delight to stroll around. It has a fascinating museum, mainly containing relics of everyday life in the Cathar settlement, such as coins and domestic utensils, but there are also remnants of some of the weapons used in the fighting around the castle during the siege, such as sword blades and the heavy stone balls that were hurled by a giant catapult against the castle walls. The museum is open all year, except in January. →

→ **The Frau Gorge** The River Hers rises in hills above Ax-les-Thermes and flows north to eventually join the River Ariège just south of Toulouse. It thus runs across the grain of the land, the successive waves of the Pyrenean foothills that lie in its path being orientated east–west. North of Comus, where the river crosses thick layers of limestone, it has carved into the rocks the stupendously deep and steep-sided Frau Gorge. The valley bottom of the gorge (and the Sentier Cathare which follows its route) drops more than 300m in a horizontal distance of hardly 2km. The most striking scenery is at the northern end of the gorge, where towering cliffs and pinnacles soar up from right alongside the riverbed.

Strollers in the Frau Gorge

STAGE 11

Montségur to Roquefixade

There is a Cathar castle at each end of this stage – Montségur and Roquefixade (so you may want to visit Roquefixade Castle today to allow time for sightseeing in Foix tomorrow). The castles sit atop their respective pinnacles and are an impressive sight from various viewpoints along the way. Impressive too are the high mountains of Ariège, on the horizon to the south.

Much of this stage is in woodland. The trail follows a switchback route, but it is not too demanding.

Distance	17km
Walking time	4 hours 15 mins (plus at least an hour to visit Montségur Castle if you didn't go there yesterday, plus another hour for Roquefixade Castle if you visit it today)
Altitude	Between 580m and 1025m
Ascent/Descent	550m/710m (plus a climb of over 150m to Montségur Castle from the trail and another of 150m to Roquefixade Castle)
IGN 1:25,000 Maps	2247OT (Lavelanet) and 2147ET (Foix Tarascon-sur-Ariège); Montségur is in map fold 2C of the Lavelanet map, Roquefixade is in map fold 4D of the Foix map

Navigation

From Montségur **(1)** up to the col **(2)** at the foot of the rock pinnacle on which Montségur Castle is situated, the Sentier Cathare coincides with the GR7B and the GR107, so the waymarking for this short section is red and white. From the col **(2)** to Roquefixade **(7)** the waymarking is red and yellow.

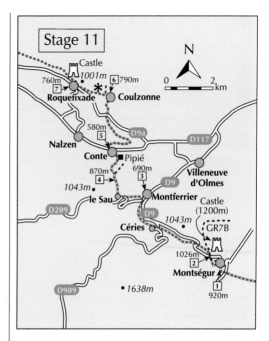

From Montségur (1) set out on the D9 as it climbs towards Montségur Castle.

The road swings sharply to the right, and the official Sentier Cathare route goes up a tarmacked lane on the left. The lane climbs quite steeply at first, then bends to the right as it enters open country. Thereafter, it climbs more gently towards the col below the steep hill on which Montségur Castle is situated, soon to meet the D9 again.

(**Note** It is quicker and no more arduous to continue along the D9 for a few metres, then take a cut-off path going up on the left (it may be signposted for the château). This path climbs through woodland and eventually comes out onto the lane that is the official Sentier Cathare route. Turn right onto the lane and you soon meet again the D9.)

Cross the D9 and follow a sunken green lane almost directly opposite. After a short distance you cross the path going up to Montségur Castle, which is now high above you, on the right. The GR107 long-distance path, which you have been following since Comus and which has coincided with the GR7B, has its terminus here **(2)**. If you now visit the castle, return afterwards to this point.

Immediately ahead is a path fork where you go left (the path going down on the right is the GR7B). The trail enters woodland and soon starts to go downhill quite steeply, eventually coming down to the D9 again, where you turn sharp right. Follow the road as it turns left. Soon afterwards, go through a wooden gate on the left and cross the open ground beyond.

The trail enters woodland again, and shortly after, be careful to follow it as it forks sharp right onto another track, descending fairly steeply towards the stream in the valley below. Parts of the next section of the path, which runs alongside – and here and there crosses – the stream, can be quite muddy, even in periods of dry weather, but the route is obvious.

View northwards from outside the walls of Montségur Castle; the foundations of the Cathars' village have been excavated here

You eventually emerge from the woodland and reach the D909, which you cross. The trail goes across a meadow, bears to the left and fords the stream that you have been following. A little further along, the trail is joined by a path coming down on the left, from Céries. Continue to follow the path down the valley. The trail soon reaches the outskirts of Montferrier and joins a tarmacked lane. At two successive crossings with other tarmacked lanes, go straight across.

Pass a campsite on the right, and just after that, turn left to cross a road bridge over a wide river and enter the centre of Montferrier **(3)**. Turn sharp left up another road (unless you want to visit the shop on the right), and after about 100m, fork uphill to the right.

Follow the lane ahead as it climbs out of the town. Where the lane bears right, carry straight on, up a wide, paved footpath that enters woodland. Go left at the first path fork, by a metal cross, then right at the second fork.

Bridge at Montferrier

When you meet a tarmacked road, go straight across. The path, still climbing, then crosses tarmac another four times. The trail meets the road yet again, and this time continues along it, straight ahead.

Now in more open country, you come to the hamlet of le Sau, where you go right at a T-junction. After passing through the hamlet, the road becomes an unsurfaced track and bears to the right, terracing high above a valley below on the right.

On reaching a col with a wooden gate on the right **(4)**, go through the gate and down the sunken, stony footpath on the left. Go through another wooden gate, enter a splendid beech forest and continue along the forest track, straight ahead.

The track turns sharp left then sharp right, descending as it does so. There is then another diversion from the former route of the trail. Watch out for and follow a footpath that turns sharp left, off the track. This path soon swings to the right, crosses a stream and starts a long descent through the forest. It crosses the stream again a couple of times, then joins another forest track.

That track emerges by a stone building marked on the 1:25,000 map as Pipié. Here, take the surfaced lane that bears to the left and continues the descent through the forest. Lower down you approach some buildings (including a restaurant, Les Sapins) at a place called Conte **(5)**, but just before you get there the trail turns sharp right onto another surfaced lane which you follow up to the busy D117.

Turn left, and you now have to follow the D117 for about 150m (the Sentier Cathare continues higher up, on the other side of the road). There are hard shoulders to walk along, but bear in mind that the traffic here can be moving pretty fast.

The trail turns sharp right, off the road, onto a track that enters woodland. It bears to the left and then begins a steady climb. Further on, after the trail passes beneath an open area on the left, it curves downhill to the left for a short distance. Bear left at successive track forks here. The trail soon resumes its climb, and runs above and to

Looking up to Roquefixade Castle, at the western end of Stage 11

the right of the open area that you passed below a few minutes previously.

The slope eventually eases off and you begin a gentle descent. The trail swings right, and a few minutes later you emerge from the forest onto the D9a. Cross this road and take another minor road, forking off the D9a to the right, and follow it up to the hamlet of Coulzonne (6). There is an especially lovely view from Coulzonne over the forests and farmland of the rolling foothills of the Pyrenees.

Follow the road through the hamlet as it turns sharp left and soon becomes an unsurfaced track. At a track fork soon afterwards, go straight ahead.

The trail passes a **memorial to members of the French Resistance**, set in a peaceful patch of open ground with a couple of benches, then continues straight ahead beyond the memorial.

After terracing across the hillside, the path starts to descend gently towards **Roquefixade**, bringing you in at its eastern end (7).

Roquefixade Castle is perched high above the village, a little way to the west (see route description for Stage 12).

Notes for west–east walkers
To pick up the Sentier Cathare on leaving the square in Roquefixade (7), go to the left of the church, then take a turning on the left and meet the lane that runs along the back of the village. Turn right along this lane, which soon becomes a grass track leading away from the village in a roughly eastward direction. You are then on the trail.

POINTS OF INTEREST

Monument near Coulzonne to French Resistance fighters killed here in 1944

Memorial to French Resistance Fighters This memorial was erected to mark the deaths of nearly 20 local members of the French Resistance, who died during an attack on nearby Coulzonne by 400 German troops and French militia. The attack took place shortly before the liberation on 6 July 1944.

Roquefixade Village In contrast to most medieval villages, which grew up in irregular fashion around a church, or extended slowly along a highway, Roquefixade was created from scratch as an entirely new settlement, hence its rectilinear plan. This happened in the 13th century, after the crusade against the Cathars, as the French kingdom consolidated its hold on the territory.

Roquefixade Castle The remains of this Cathar castle may be scant, but they occupy one of the most impressive positions in the whole region. Access to the site is unobstructed and without charge, but, as a notice in the village says, the castle is a '*site vertigineux*' and should be approached with '*prudence*'.

Roquefixade Castle was a stronghold of Cathar society in the early 13th century, but played no significant role during the crusade against the Cathars. However, after the crushing of the Cathars, the French took over Roquefixade Castle and installed a garrison here, and the castle became part of the line of fortifications defending the then southern frontier of France. But in 1632 the French king ordered it to be demolished, and this was done with meticulous care. Its remains have been crumbling into ruin ever since.

STAGE 12

Roquefixade to Foix

As you head west on this stage, there may be final glimpses of Montségur, far to the east, and almost certainly splendid views back to Roquefixade Castle, looking ready to totter from its precipitous perch. But the most impressive panorama – and the grand finale of the whole trek – comes as a reward shortly before the end of the trail, when you gaze down on the three-towered stronghold of Foix castle. It looks today as massive and impregnable as it ever was.

So, three Cathar castles in one stage. But that's not all – the trail passes through forests with tall, slender beech trees of regal proportion, and the contrast between this cool, green, humid Atlantic forest and the dry, hot, richly scented *garrigue* plateau at the eastern, Mediterranean end of the trail could hardly be greater. There is also the wide, majestic Ariège valley to admire, and of course the Pyrenees stretching away to the far distance. If you haven't already done so, you will surely want to return one day to make their closer acquaintance.

Distance	18km
Walking time	5 hours
Altitude	Between 370m and 930m (or to just over 1000m if the alternative route described below is taken)
Ascent/Descent	500m/890m
IGN 1:25,000 Map	2147ET (Foix Tarascon-sur-Ariège); Roquefixade is in map fold 4D, Foix is in map fold 2C

Navigation

This stage carries red and yellow waymarks along its whole length, but there are one or two diversions away from the waymarked Sentier Cathare route which are worth taking. These are described below.

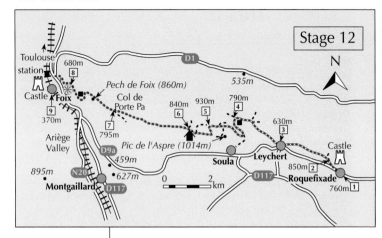

From the upper end of the square in Roquefixade **(1)**, head west – i.e. towards the castle and away from the church. A stony track takes you out of the village and starts to climb. It passes immediately below the crag on which are perched the remains of Roquefixade Castle.

Steps on the right mark the start of a steep path that leads to the castle, but the Sentier Cathare itself continues straight ahead. After a short distance you come to a track fork **(2)** where you turn left. The track descends and you come to another fork. Go left again and follow the track as it curves to the right, then traverses an open hillside.

The trail starts to descend and swings to the left a little. At the bottom of the slope, leave the track, which curves to the right, and follow a line across the grassy col straight ahead.

When you reach an intersection with a stony track, turn left and follow this track, which soon swings to the right and goes down the hillside towards the village of Leychert. You emerge in the upper part of that village **(3)**. The trail turns right and follows a tarmacked road for a short while, then forks to the right of a fine old stone building. It then follows a wide farm track that climbs steadily away from the village.

Roquefixade Castle, with the Pyrenees of Ariège in the far distance

On your left is a pretty valley, the head of which you will cross later on. Eventually the trail comes to a junction of several tracks – turn left here and follow the trail as it terraces across the hillside. At a T-junction **(4)** be careful to go down to the left and cross the valley. The trail swings sharply to the right, then climbs and swings left. It passes to the right of, first a handsome stone building (marked on the IGN 1:25,000 map as Charillon), then a large, modern farm building.

Further on, continue straight ahead where a forest road goes off to the sharp right, but immediately afterwards take a rougher track that also goes off sharp right.

You then have a stiff climb through the forest. At the top of this steep section, the trail threads its way across semi-open country. After passing alongside old stone walls, it meets another track, where you turn left.

Alternative Route

A little further along there is a well-used path going up the hillside on the left. It is an alternative route on a local walking circuit, and well worth taking. The path climbs steadily through the forest, then bears to the right. It goes down a little and emerges onto open ground just to the right of the Pic de l'Aspre (1014m) – from here a most wonderful panorama towards the Ariège Mountains appears. The alternative route continues on the right, descending the hill and following the edge of the woodland on the right. Eventually it re-enters woodland, then soon meets the current route of the Sentier Cathare. Here, if you have followed this alternative route, you should turn left.

From the point where the alternative route (above) first turns off to the left, the current route of the Sentier Cathare carries straight on, along a grassy track. This track soon descends to meet a well-made forest road coming up on the right. Turn left, then follow the forest road through a stretch of fine beech forest. At the top of an incline you reach the Pas du Falcou **(5)**. Here, turn left onto a track which is at first quite stony underfoot.

Where the trail bears round to the right, the alternative route mentioned above comes in on the left. The path you are now following descends through semi-open ground, then comes to an open field. Go straight across the field and re-enter the forest on the other side. Be careful with all the turns that follow, because the way-marking hereabouts may not be very clear.

Bear round to the right, then come down to meet a wide forest road descending from the right. Go down that road to the left. You pass to the right of a small, unlocked refuge in the forest.

The trail arrives at an opening, with one forest road going down on the right and another straight ahead **(6)**. Go straight ahead, passing a metal road barrier, and keep to this forest road for a considerable distance. It is easy to follow, and for most of the way you have a splendid beech forest on both sides. You climb steadily at first, then descend and eventually reach the Col de Porte Pa **(7)**.

Looking north down the valley of the River Ariège, from high ground above Foix

Go through a gate, and follow the Sentier Cathare as it winds up the steep slope straight ahead. Towards the upper part of the climb, you come out into open country again. Where the slope levels out and the track forks, go right. This takes you to the right of the ridge crest, with views now to the north over the outer foothills of the Pyrenees.

The trail descends a little to the left, crossing the crest of the ridge. Then, where the track that you are on swings to the right and goes through a line of trees, the Sentier Cathare takes the path that branches off sharply to the left. (You may see a home-made sign on a tree pointing left, towards Foix – if so, that confirms the direction you should be taking.)

The path, now in semi-woodland, descends to the right, and you soon reach the top corner of a sizeable but ruined, stone-built farmstead (marked on the 1:25,000 map as the Pech de Naut). The path goes across the open ground in front of the ruins, down a short embankment, then turns to go half-right. The trail traverses semi-open ground, gently descending the slope of the hill ahead.

You eventually come to a corner of a fence enclosing a field below on the left. The route goes half-right, again downhill, to enter semi-woodland and go under a power line. Keep an eye open now for a well-used but unwaymarked path forking off to the left **(8)**, just before the Sentier Cathare turns to the right, and where, a few metres on the right, there is a pylon along the power line. This path will take you along a rocky spur of land to an eagle's-nest viewpoint that directly overlooks **Foix**, **Foix Castle** and the **Ariège Valley**. Later, return to the Sentier Cathare and turn left along it.

The trail bears right, then sharp left, and the path becomes quite stony and descends more steeply, bending to the right as it does so. Mostly enclosed by woodland, it passes through a wooden gate en route.

As you begin to approach the foot of the hill, you will see Foix railway station down on the right. Eventually you come to a point where the path forks – the Sentier Cathare goes to the right.

The final signpost on the Sentier Cathare, near Foix town centre

RUE
SAINTE RAPINE

GRP
SENTIER CATHARE

LE PECH 2H15

(**Note** The unwaymarked path to the left offers a more exciting (and shorter) final descent into Foix. After a steep descent, this path suddenly emerges above gardens and houses that are themselves just above the River Ariège – Foix and its castle lie on the other side. The path then winds down to go underneath the houses and emerges on a main road alongside the river and railway line. The Pont Vieux opposite leads into the centre of the town.)

From the path fork the Sentier Cathare descends to the right, goes through another wooden gate, and at the bottom turns left onto a lane that enters the outskirts of the town. At the end of the lane, turn left onto a road called the Rue Sainte Rapine, which eventually brings you down to a main road. Cross onto the other side and turn left along this road (unless you want to go directly to the station, which is on the right).

You soon reach the Pont Vieux, which marks the western end of the Sentier Cathare (**9**).

Notes for west–east walkers

Those who set off on the Sentier Cathare from Foix, and who have shared with the author the experience of arriving for the first time in a large town (Guildford, for example) and of having to take a compass bearing down the main street to find the way to the long-distance path which leads out of the town (the North Downs Way in the instance given), will understand the importance of paying particular attention to navigation through the initial, built-up section of the trail.

Remember that after leaving Foix you face one of the stiffest climbs along the whole trail – nearly 500m in a distance of only 4km. During that climb, be careful on a winding, slightly obscure section of the trail near the ruined farmstead that is shown on the 1:25,000 map as the Pech de Naut.

POINTS OF INTEREST

Foix Castle and Museum Foix Castle sits on a vertical-sided rock outcrop, guarding a pass through the Ariège Valley. It offers today one of the most powerful and well-known images of Cathar castle country.

The Count of Foix was one of Simon de Montfort's most formidable opponents. His sympathies were clearly with the Cathars (his sister Esclarmonde was herself a Bonne Femme), and his principal sanctuary was the castle of Foix. De Montfort never took it by force, but as he became ever more threatening and powerful, the Count of Foix made a tactical retreat. He handed over his castle to the Pope's legate in 1215, and as a military threat to de Montfort, Foix Castle was thus neutralised.

Foix Castle, still high and mighty, as it was in the age of the Cathars

De Montfort now seemed invincible, but the people of Languedoc continued to inflict setbacks on the occupying army. This culminated in de Montfort being killed during a skirmish just outside Toulouse in June 1218, and in the same year the Count of Foix had little trouble in recovering his castle.

However, the crusade was rekindled with devastating force, and just over 10 years later the Count of Foix finally submitted to the King of France. The castle was spared, but it was never again a refuge for the Cathars.

From the castle's high battlements there is a glorious view over Foix and up the Ariège Valley, and inside there is a museum, devoted mainly to archaeology and military history. The castle and museum are open to the public on most days throughout the year, although the days and times of opening in the winter months are a little more restricted than in summer. →

→ **Foix Town Centre** The narrow streets and crowded-together buildings in the centre of Foix, below the castle, testify to the town's medieval origin. There are several attractive timber-framed houses, and fountains and squares. To the north of the castle is St-Volusien church, where there was once a powerful abbey. The church was seriously damaged during religious wars in the 16th century, and has been reconstructed since then. Its interior is spacious and elegant.

The Ariège Valley This wide, handsome valley is a principal artery of communication between the plains to the north, in which lie Pamiers and Toulouse, and the high mountains and Spain to the south. This is where the Cathar church in 13th-century Languedoc had its strongest following. Its followers escaped up the valley, heading for the Pyrenean cols that led them away from their French persecutors.

The author, conserving energy before tackling the final descent to Foix (below); (photo by Wendy Mattingly)

FINAL THOUGHTS

The end of the Sentier Cathare has been reached. What impressions remain?

Each traveller will have his or her own memories. But these may well include recollections of sun-baked vineyards and shady forests. Of buzzards circling in air currents high above. Of blazing sunsets and torrential downpours. Of thirsty arrivals and chilly, early-morning departures. Of warm welcomes and cool white wine in sleepy village squares. Of stunning panoramas and the sweet taste of wild strawberries. And of wild flowers in profusion on lofty grass plateaus.

A pressing desire to return and explore the snow-topped mountains that have almost constantly been in view to the south may also figure.

But the clearest recollections will surely include the sight of each of the Cathar castles encountered along the way. On the main route of the Sentier Cathare there are nine in total, each with its own unique character, and every one dominating the landscape in which it is set and drawing the onlooker's eye with irresistible force.

Of those nine Cathar castles, one stands out. It is the one with the closest connections to the Cathars, the one that, more than any other monument, has come to symbolise the Cathars' faith, self-sacrifice and fanaticism. It is where the most tragic event in their century-long tragedy took place. It is of course Montségur.

It is true that the burning alive of more than 200 men, women and children at the foot of Montségur Castle in 1244 was an event of no great historical moment. The movement of history's tectonic plates that was provoked by the crusade against the Cathars had settled down long before the surrender of Montségur. Languedoc had irretrievably become part of France, and the Inquisition had been set on its merciless path, and would be used to suppress heresy and dissent throughout the Christian world for centuries to come. Even had they survived, the Cathars of Montségur could have done nothing to alter any of that.

*Monument below
Montségur Castle to
the Cathars executed
there in 1244*

But the nature of their heroic last stand – and the fact that records of it have miraculously survived – means that Montségur is today a powerful symbol of man's inhumanity to man. It is an image of what we like to think has been confined to the past, and of what we certainly want to keep out of our present and out of our children's future. That – together with the awe-inspiring landscape of Montségur and the mysteries that the place still guards – is perhaps what attract so many visitors to the site every year. For these reasons, a trek along the Sentier Cathare is, above all, a pilgrimage to Montségur.

To walk the Sentier Cathare is a most agreeable and satisfying outdoor experience, but it is also an encounter with the lessons of history. Those who undertake the journey are left with images and reasons for reflection that will remain vivid in their memories for the rest of their lives.

APPENDIX 1
Accommodation and Further Information

The details of the hotels, bed and breakfasts, *gîtes d'étape* and campsites listed below have been assembled from various sources, including tourist publications, websites and personal experience. This is not a comprehensive list of accommodation along the Sentier Cathare, nor can it be completely up to date (in particular, e-mail addresses and website names can change quickly and often), but it is a longer list of accommodation on the trail than appears to have been published anywhere else so far, so it should be sufficient to get you started on your pre-trek preparations.

The tourist offices and town halls (*mairies*) listed will often be able to provide further information about accommodation, shops, taxis, buses, luggage-carrying services and other facilities in their localities. They can also provide information about castles and other monuments and places of interest. Many of them now have websites and e-mail addresses.

Most of the towns and villages listed have shops, such as a baker (*boulangerie*) and a grocery store (*épicerie*), and bars and/or cafés. Larger places also have restaurants and post offices, but **places where there are likely to be no shops or bars (or very few) are marked *****.

The main towns (Port-la-Nouvelle, Sigean, St-Paul-de-Fenouillet, Quillan and Foix) have a full range of shops and services, including banks. Those towns are also accessible by public transport.

CH stands for *chambres d'hôte*, usually equivalent to a small, family-run hotel or bed and breakfast.

Five-digit numbers in brackets, for example (11360), give the postal code for the town or village to which the number refers. So, for instance, to write to the l'Amandier Hotel in Durban-Corbières at the end of Stage 1, address your letter to:

Hôtel l'Amandier
Avenue des Corbières
11360 Durban-Corbières
France

Stage 1 Port-la-Nouvelle to Durban-Corbières
Port-la-Nouvelle (11210)
Hôtel Le Méditerranée, Front de Mer, tel (00 33) (0) 4 68 48 03 08, www.hotelmediterranee.com
Le Casimir (hotel), Avenue de la Mer, tel (00 33) (0) 4 68 48 33 88, Catherine.Casimir@wanadoo.fr, www.lecasimir.com
Camping Cap du Roc, Route de Lapalme, tel (00 33) (0) 4 68 48 00 98, capduroc@aol.com
Camping Municipal du Golf, Boulevard Francis-Vals, tel (00 33) (0) 4 68 48 08 42
Camping Côte Vermeille, Chemin des Vignes, tel (00 33) (0) 4 68 4805 80, infos@complexe-cote-vermeille.com
Office de Tourisme, Place Paul Valéry BP 20, 11210 Port-la-Nouvelle Cedex, tel (00 33) (0) 4 68 48 00 51, officedetourisme.portlanouvelle@wanadoo.fr, www.portlanouvelle.com.

Sigean (11130) (2km northwest of the trail)

CH (F Leclerq), 36 Rue de la Liberté, tel (00 33) (0) 4 68 11 40 70

Hôtel le Saint Anne, 3 Avenue Michel de l'Hospital, tel (00 33) (0) 4 68 48 24 38, lesaintanne@ataraxie.fr

Office de Tourisme, Place de la Libération, 11130 Sigean, tel (00 33) (0) 4 68 48 14 81, sigean@wanadoo.fr www.sigean.org

Roquefort-des-Corbières (11540)

CH La Maison des Iles, 23bis Rue de l'Esplandidou, tel (00 33) (0) 4 68 48 20 86

CH Zénaïde, 27 Rue des Chasseurs, tel (00 33) (0) 4 68 48 66 09

Mairie, tel (00 33) (0) 4 68 48 20 47

Durban-Corbières (11360)

CH Le Clos des Rosalines, Avenue des Corbières, tel (00 33) (0) 4 68 11 40 70

Hôtel l'Amandier, Avenue des Corbières, tel (00 33) (0) 4 68 45 89 48

Camping Municipal Les Platanes, tel (00 33) (0) 4 68 45 06 81

Mairie, tel (00 33) (0) 4 68 45 90 12

Stage 2 Durban-Corbières to Tuchan
Embres-et-Castelmaure (11360) ***

CH L'Embresienne, 11 Route de Villeneuve, tel (00 33) (0) 4 68 45 81 74

Mairie, tel (00 33) (0) 4 68 45 91 61

Aguilar Castle, tel (00 33) (0) 4 68 45 51 00 (mairie, Tuchan)

Tuchan (11350)

Gîte d'étape St-Roch (2km northwest of Tuchan), Route de Fasre, tel (00 33) (0) 4 68 45 47 91

CH (Ancienne Gendarmerie), 9 Rue du Pont, tel 06 07 10 61 47

CH Le Clos des Oliviers, Route de Narbonne, tel (00 33) (0) 4 68 45 51 04, joelmartin.2@free.fr

CH Lou Prat, 11 Rue de la Poste, tel (00 33) (0) 4 68 45 46 47, joachim.herrero@freesbee.fr

Hostellerie (hotel) du Mont Tauch, 10 Avenue de la Gare, tel (00 33) (0) 4 68 45 49 90

Camping Le Relais d'Aguilar, tel (00 33) (0) 4 68 45 47 84, relaisaguilar@wanadoo.fr

Camping La Peiriere, tel (00 33) (0) 4 68 45 46 50, lapeiriere@caramail.com

Office de Tourisme, L'Office Intercommunal de Tourisme des Hautes Corbières, Route de Padern, 11350 Cucugnan, tel (00 33) (0) 4 68 45 69 40, www.ot-hautescorbieres.com

Stage 3 Tuchan to Duilhac-sous-Peyrepertuse
Padern (11350)

Gîte d'étape, 3 Rue de l'Affenage, tel (00 33) (0) 4 68 45 40 58

CH La Fleurine, Rue Tranquille, tel (00 33) (0) 4 68 45 01 03

CH (the *épicerie*, grocery store), 9 Rue du Conflent, tel 04 68 33 44 98

Office de Tourisme – as for Tuchan (Stage 2)

Quéribus Castle, tel (00 33) (0) 4 68 45 03 69 (this is the number for the mairie in
Cucugnan, as well as for information about the 'pocket theatre' in the village)

Cucugnan (11350)

CH L'Amandière, 3 Chemin de la Chapelle, tel (00 33) (0) 4 68 45 43 42
CH Les Santolines, 3 Rue Alphonse-Daudet, tel (00 33) (0) 4 68 45 00 04
CH (M-J Séguy), 3 Chemin de la Chapelle, tel (00 33) (0) 4 68 45 43 42
Auberge du Vigneron, 2 Rue Achille-Mir, tel (00 33) (0) 4 68 45 03 00, www.auberge-
vigneron.com
Auberge de Cucugnan, 2 Place de la Fontaine, tel (00 33) (0) 4 68 45 40 84
Office de Tourisme – as for Tuchan (Stage 2)

Duilhac-sous-Peyrepertuse (11350)

Gîte d'étape, 18 Rue de la Fontaine, tel (00 33) (0) 4 68 45 01 74, gite.duilhac@wanadoo.fr
CH/*Gîtes d'étape* Bugamus, tel (00 33) (0) 4 68 64 34 42
Auberge du Vieux Moulin (opposite the Auberge de la Source), 24 Rue de la Fontaine, tel
(00 33) (0) 4 68 45 02 17
Office de Tourisme – as for Tuchan (Stage 2)

Stage 4 Duilhac-sous-Peyrepertuse to Prugnanes, and Stage 4 (North Variant) Duilhac-sous-Peyrepertuse to Camps-sur-l'Agly

Peyrepertuse Castle, tel (00 33) (0) 6 71 58 63 36 for information about the castle and to
make bookings for guided tours, or visit chateau.peyrepertuse@wanadoo.fr

St-Paul-de-Fenouillet (66220) (2km south of the trail)

CH Le Pastadou, 42 Avenue Jean Moulin, tel (00 33) (0) 4 68 25 21
CH La Posada, 3 Avenue Léon Blum, tel (00 33) (0) 4 68 82 01 71, www.la-posada-po.com
La Désirade, Chemin la Boulzane, tel (00 33) (0) 4 68 35 28 81, www.la-
desirade.oxatis.com
Hôtel Le Relais des Corbières, tel (00 33) (0) 4 68 59 23 69
Hôtel Le Châtelet (2km west of St-Paul, on D117), tel (00 33) (0) 4 68 59 01 20
Villa des Pins, 8 Rue du Pont de la Fou (south of St-Paul on D619), tel (00 33) (0) 4 68 59
24 43, www.lavilladespins.com
Camping Camp de l'Agly, tel (00 33) (0) 4 68 59 09 09, contact@camping-agly.com
Office de Tourisme, Boulevard de l'Agly, tel (00 33) (0) 4 68 59 07 57, contact@st-
paul66.com, www.st-paul66.com

Prugnanes (66220) ***

Gîte d'étape, 7 Avenue des Fenouillèdes, tel (00 33) (0) 4 68 59 23 35 (or (00 33) (0) 4 68
59 10 30 – mairie)
CH Domaine de Coussères (2km southeast of Prugnanes on D20), tel (00 33) (0) 4 68 59
23 55, www.cousseres.com

Cubières-sur-Cinoble (11190) ***

CH Le Saouzé, tel (00 33) (0) 4 68 31 61 55

CH Accueil au Village, tel (00 33) (0) 4 68 69 84 17, leroy.francoise@accueilauvillage.fr

Mairie, tel (00 33) (0) 4 68 69 88 64, mairie.secretariat@cubieres-sur-cinoble.fr,
www.cubieres-sur-cinoble.fr.fm

Camps-sur-l'Agly (11190) ***

Gîte d'étape (and campsite) La Ferme de Camps, 1 Rue du Château, tel (00 33) (0) 4 68 69
87 53, jean-pierre.clervoix@wanadoo.fr

Gîte d'étape La Bastide (2km west of Camps, but on the trail), tel (00 33) (0) 4 68 69 87 57

CH Maison du Chevalier, 1 Rue de la *Mairie*, tel (00 33) (0) 4 68 69 83 90, arienne1@hot-mail.com

Mairie, tel (00 33) (0) 4 68 69 87 50 agly@fr.fm, see also www.pays-de-couiza.com

Stage 5 Prugnanes to Puilaurens, and Stage 5 (North Variant) Camps-sur-l'Agly to Bugarach
Caudiès-de-Fenouillèdes (66220)

Gîte d'étape, tel (00 33) (0) 4 68 59 92 25 (mairie)

CH (P Jouret), Avenue de Roussillon, tel (00 33) (0) 4 68 59 91 97

CH Cave Ancienne, tel (00 33) (0) 4 68 59 95 50

Camping Castel Fizel, tel (00 33) (0) 4 68 59 92 94

Mairie, tel (00 33) (0) 4 68 59 92 25, www.mairie-caudies-fenouilledes.fr

Lapradelle and Puilaurens (11140) (Shops and eating places are mainly at Lapradelle, 1km north of Puilaurens.)

Gîte d'étape Aigues-Bonnes (3km east of Puilaurens, on the trail), tel (00 33) (0) 4 68 20 51 90

CH Mas Occitan (just south of Puilaurens, on the D22), tel (00 33) (0) 4 68 20 66 09

CH Maison 1800, 6 Place des Tilleuls, Lapradelle, tel (00 33) (0) 4 68 20 79 66, www.maison1800.com

Hôtel Le Viaduc, Lapradelle, tel (00 33) (0) 4 68 20 53 01

Mairie, tel (00 33) (0) 4 68 20 52 07

Bugarach (11190) *** (Occasional, but not daily, travelling shops; restaurant.)

Gîte d'étape La Maison de la Nature et de la Randonnée, tel (00 33) (0) 4 68 69 83 88 (or 04 68 69 86 72 (mairie))

CH Le Presbytère, tel (00 33) (0) 4 68 69 82 12

Mairie, tel (00 33) (0) 4 68 69 86 72, mairie@bugarach.fr, www.bugarach.fr, see also
www.pays-de-couiza.com

Stage 6 Puilaurens to Quirbajou (or Labeau), and Stage 6 (North Variant) Bugarach and Quillan
Puilaurens Castle

Accueil du Château, 11140 Lapradelle-Puilaurens, tel (00 33) (0) 4 68 20 65 26,
info@lapradelle-puilaurens.com, www.lapradelle-puilaurens.com

Axat (11140)

Gîte d'étape (and campsite) La Crémade (2km northeast of Axat, close to the trail), tel (00 33) (0) 4 68 20 50 64

Gîte d'étape Axat, tel (00 33) (0) 4 68 20 53 34

Auberge La Petite Ourse, 16 Route Départementale, tel (00 33) (0) 4 68 20 59 20

CH Le Rébenty (at the junction of the D117 and D107 – off the trail, but usefully situated on bus route between Axat and Quillan), tel (00 33) (0) 4 68 20 50 78, info@lerebenty.com, www.lerebenty.com

Camping du Pont d'Aliès (1km northeast of Axat), tel (00 33) (0) 4 68 20 53 27

Maison des Pyrénées du Pays Cathare (tourist information office for the Axat region), Rond-point d'Aliès (at junction of D117 and D118, 1km north-ast of Axat), tel (00 33) (0) 4 68 20 59 61, cdc-axat@wanadoo.fr

Quirbajou (11500) ***

Gîte d'étape/CH El Cadet, tel (00 33) (0) 4 68 20 53 91

Mairie, tel (00 33) (0) 4 68 20 64 27

Labeau (2km west of Marsa) (11140) ***

Gîte d'étape/CH, tel (00 33) (0) 4 68 20 54 12

Mairie (Marsa), tel (00 33) (0) 4 68 20 55 53

Quillan (11500)

Gîte d'étape (and campsite) La Forge (1km south of Quillan), tel (00 33) (0) 4 68 20 23 79, laforge.quillan@wanadoo.fr

CH L'Assaladou, Chemin de Fauruc, tel (00 33) (0) 4 68 11 40 70

There are several hotels in Quillan, including:

Hôtel Canal, 36 Boulevard Charles de Gaulle, tel (00 33) (0) 4 68 20 08 62, hotelcanal@ataraxie.fr, www.hotel-canal.com

Hôtel Cartier, 31 Boulevard Charles de Gaulle, tel (00 33) (0) 4 68 20 05 14, hotel.cartier@ataraxie.fr, www.hotelcartier.com

Camping La Sapinette, Rue René-Delpech, tel (00 33) (0) 4 68 20 13 52

Quillan Tourist Office, Maison du Tourisme 'Aude en Pyrénées', Square André Tricoire, 11500 Quillan, tel (00 33) (0) 4 68 20 07 78, tourisme.quillan@wanadoo.fr, www.ville-quillan.fr

Stage 7 Quirbajou (or Labeau) to Puivert, and Stage 7 (North Variant) Quillan to Puivert

Nébias (11500)

Gîte d'étape L'Assaladou (1km north of Nébias), tel (00 33) (0) 4 68 20 80 89

Le Thury, 66 Allée de la Promenade (CH, restaurant, bar, *épicerie*), tel (00 33) (0) 4 68 20 82 20, esra.bolher@wanadoo.fr

Camping Fontaulie-Sud, tel (00 33) (0) 4 68 20 17 62, lefontauliesud@free.fr

Mairie, tel (00 33) (0) 4 68 20 06 13, mairienebias@cbhouse.fr

Puivert Castle, tel (00 33) (0) 4 68 20 81 52, infos@chateau-de-puivert.com, www.chateau-de-puivert.com

Puivert (11230)

Gîte d'étape Relais des Marionnettes, 19 Route 117, tel (00 33) (0) 4 68 20 80 69, michel.dubrunfaut@wanadoo.fr

CH L'Irénée, 2 Rue du Chemin de Ronde, tel (00 33) (0) 4 68 20 95 79, www.irenee-puivert.com

CH La Peyrouse, Route des Tougnets, tel (00 33) (0) 4 68 20 24 19; lapeyrousepuivert@yahoo.fr

CH Au Petit Verger, 8 Route Départementale, tel (00 33) (0) 4 68 20 66 08, martyn.pickering@wanadoo.fr, www.puivertaccommodation.com

Camping de Fontclaire, tel (00 33) (0)04 68 20 00 58, mairie.puivert@libertysurf.fr

Mairie, 2 Place de l'Eglise, tel (00 33) (0) 4 68 20 08 04, mairie.puivert@libertysurf.fr, www.puivert.net

Musée du Quercorb, 16, Rue Barry du Lion, 11230 Puivert, tel (00 33) (0)04 68 20 80 98, musee.quercorb@wanadoo.fr

See also: www.quercorb.com

Stage 8 Puivert to Espezel (or Belvis)
Espezel (11340)

Gîte d'étape, tel (00 33) (0) 4 68 20 72 89

Hôtel Grau, tel (00 33) (0) 4 68 20 30 14, hotel.grau@wanadoo.fr

Camping Le Calcat, tel (00 33) (0) 4 68 20 30 34

Musée Paysan, 123 Rue du Moulin, tel (00 33) (0) 4 68 20 38 17

Belvis (11340)

Gîte d'étape La Font Blanche (2km west of Belvis), tel (00 33) (0) 4 68 20 33 70

Gîte d'étape La Gineste (1km southwest of Belvis), tel (00 33) (0) 4 68 20 76 31, pascal.chenal@laposte.nett

CH Le Petit Jardin, tel (00 33) (0) 4 68 20 98 39, parsleylowe@hotmail.com www.cafebelvis.com (in English)

CH l'Hom à Courtois, tel (00 33) (0) 4 68 31 70 02

Mairie, tel (00 33) (0) 4 68 20 37 62

Office de Tourisme du Pays de Sault, Route d'Ax les Thermes, 11340 Belcaire, tel (00 33) (0) 4 68 20 75 89, o.t.p.s@wanadoo.fr, www.paysdesault.com

Stage 9 Espezel (or Belvis) to Comus
Comus (11340) *** (Occasional, but not daily, travelling shops)

Gîte d'étape, tel (00 33) (0) 4 68 20 33 69, anne@gites-comus.com

Camurac (3km southeast of Comus on D20 road) (11340)

Gîte/CH Les Sapins, tel (00 33) (0) 4 68 31 32 01, www.lessapins-camurac.com

Gîte/CH La Marmite, tel (00 33) (0) 4 68 20 73 31

Auberge du Pays de Sault, tel (00 33) (0) 4 68 20 32 09

Camping Les Sapins, tel (00 33) (0) 4 68 20 38 11, camping@lessapins-camurac.com

Office de Tourisme – as for Stage 8

On Montaillou, see www.mairie-montaillou.fr

Stage 10 Comus to Montségur

Montségur (09300)

Gîte d'étape, tel (00 33) (0) 5 61 01 08 57, infos@gite-montsegur.com

CH L'Oustal, tel (00 33) (0) 5 61 02 80 70, serge.germa@wanadoo.fr

CH Serre de Marou (2km northwest of Montségur, off the D9, but close to the trail), tel (00 33) (0) 5 61 01 14 75

Hôtel Costes, tel (00 33) (0) 5 61 01 10 24

Camping Municipal, tel (00 33) (0) 5 61 01 10 27

Office du Tourisme, 09300 Montségur, tel (00 33) (0) 5 61 03 03 03, info.tourisme@montsegur.org, www.montsegur.org

Montségur mairie, tel (00 33) (0) 5 61 01 10 27, mairie.montsegur@wanadoo.fr, www.citaenet.com/montsegur

Montségur Castle (guided tours) and Museum, tel (00 33) (0) 5 61 01 06 94, guide.montsegur@wanadoo.fr

For Stages 10 and 11, see also www.paysdolmes.org

Stage 11 Montségur to Roquefixade
Montferrier (09300)

Gîte d'étape La Freychède, tel (00 33) (0) 5 61 01 10 38, freychede@wanadoo.fr

Gîte d'étape Le Paquetayre, tel (00 33) (0) 5 61 03 06 29

Camping Municipal, tel (00 33) (0) 5 61 01 20 97

Montferrier Museum, tel (00 33) (0) 5 61 01 91 47

Roquefixade (09300) *** (drinks at the village gîte)

Gîte d'étape (village), tel (00 33) (0) 5 61 03 02 25, ppleran09@aol.com, gite-etape-roquefixade.com

Gîte d'étape, Le Relais des Pogs (1km northwest of Roquefixade), tel (00 33) (0) 5 61 01 14 50, chevret.brigitte.gite.etape@wanadoo.fr

CH La Bastida dels Catars, tel 00 33 (0) 5 61 01 95 99, marisderoquefixade.com (This establishment, on the trail at the eastern entry to village, is run by Yves Maris, who is both Mayor of Roquefixade and an expert on the Cathars.)

Hôtel Le Relais des Trois Châteaux (2km southwest of Roquefixade on the D117), tel 00 33 (0) 5 61 01 33 99

For Stages 10 and 11, see also www.paysdolmes.org

Stage 12 Roquefixade to Foix
Foix (09000)

Auberge de Jeunesse (youth hostel), 16 Rue Peyrevidal, tel 00 33 (0) 5 61 65 09 04, leolagrange-foix@wanadoo.fr

Hôtel Lons (alongside the River Ariège, close to where the Sentier Cathare ends), 6 Place G-Dutilh, tel 00 33 (0) 5 34 09 28 00, hotel-lons-foix@wanadoo.fr

Camping Le Lac, tel 00 33 (0) 5 61 65 11 58, camping.du.lac@wanadoo.fr

Office de Tourisme du Pays de Foix, 29 Rue Delcassé, BP 20, 09001 Foix, tel (00 33) (0) 5 61 65 12 12, foix.tourisme@wanadoo.fr, www.ot-foix.fr

Foix Castle and Museum, tel (00 33) (0) 5 34 09 83 83

APPENDIX 2

Useful Addresses and Websites, Taxi Services

Useful Addresses and Websites
French Travel Centre, 178 Piccadilly, London W1V OAL, tel 09068 244123, info@mdlf.co.uk; www.franceguide.com

Addresses for the tourism headquarters of the Aude and Ariège *départements* are as follows (they can also supply – and they list on their websites – the addresses and other details of all the local tourist information offices in their *départements*).

Comité Départemental du Tourisme de l'Aude, Conseil Général, 11855 Carcassonne Cedex 9, tel (00 33) (0) 4 68 11 66 00, documentation@aude-tourisme.com, www.audetourisme.com.

Comité Départemental du Tourisme Ariège Pyrénées, 31 bis, Avenue du Général du Gaulle BP143, 09004 Foix Cedex, tel (00 33) (0) 5 61 02 30 70, tourisme.ariege.pyrenees@wanadoo.fr, www.ariegepyrenees.com.

Fédération Française de la Randonnée Pédestre, 14 Rue Riquet, 75019 Paris, tel (00 33) (0)1 44 89 93 90, passion.rando@ffrandonnee.fr, www.ffrandonnee.fr.

In Carcassonne you will find the Point Info-Rando FFRP Aude (Maison de Tourisme Vert, 78 ter, Rue Barbacane, 11000 Carcassonne, tel (00 33) (0) 4 68 47 69 26, ffrp@carcazssonne.fr). This is a useful source of information about walks in Aude. In particular, the FFRP in Aude has an accommodation list for places along the GR36 in the department.

If you are surfing the Internet for information about Cathars and Cathar castles, a good starting point is www.cathars.org. This website is entirely in French, and at first sight looks a bit eccentric, but once you get into it you will find that it is a good source of information about, for example, castle opening times, prices of entry, and relevant addresses, telephone numbers and websites. It also has several illustrations and plans of the castles. Also good, and in English, is www.languedoc-france.info.

Taxi Services
Some of these operators also offer baggage-transporting services for long-distance path walkers.

Eastern Sections of the Trail

Taxi Cathare (Tuchan), tel (00 33) (0) 4 68 45 45 87

Balade Cathare (Rouffiac-des-Corbières, near Peyrepertuse Castle), tel (00 33) (0) 4 68 45 05 10

Taxis Claret (St-Paul-de-Fenouillet), tel (00 33) (0) 4 68 59 29 48

Central Sections of the Trail

Allo Jacky (Quillan), tel (00 33) (0) 4 68 20 01 92

Taxi Ragnère (Quillan), tel (00 33) (0) 4 68 20 15 46

Western Sections of the Trail (Lavelanet/Montségur)

Taxi Ollivier, tel (00 33) (0) 5 61 01 13 94

Taxi Guiraud, tel (00 33) (0) 5 61 01 06 45

Passe Montagne, tel (00 33) (0) 4 68 20 38 58

APPENDIX 3

Other Long-Distance Paths in the Cathar Region

Overview

Other national long-distance walking routes in the Cathar region are shown in the Location Map on pages 8 and 9.

The **Canal du Midi** runs east–west across the northern part of the Cathar region. Its towpath is not a designated long-distance path, but it can certainly be used as one.

Otherwise, waymarked national long-distance paths in Cathar castle country (apart from the Sentier Cathare) are **GR paths** (*sentiers de Grande Randonnée*).

Waymarks showing the routes of GR paths are small red and white rectangles. Each GR path traverses a large part of France, and for the most part they are high-quality, well-maintained long-distance paths. Their routes are depicted on IGN maps, including its 1:25,000 maps. Accommodation, refreshment and supplies can readily be found at frequent intervals along most sections of most GR paths.

Many GR paths are described in detail in FFRP publications called *topo-guides*. However, some sections of certain GR paths are not currently the subject of *topo-guides*, even though they are waymarked on the ground and may also be shown on IGN maps at various scales.

Unfortunately, *topo-guides* are not at present available for most sections of GR paths in the Cathar castle region. *Topo-guides* are only available for the GR107, the GR36 south of about Peyrepertuse Castle and the GR7 north of Bram (see Appendix 4). The GR77, the GR36 north of about Peyrepertuse Castle and the GR7 south of Bram are not currently the subject of *topo-guides*, but they are waymarked on the ground.

GR paths have been created by the Fédération Française de la Randonnée Pédestre (FFRP), the equivalent in France of the Ramblers' Association. FFRP volunteers play an important role in waymarking, signposting and maintaining these excellent routes.

Regional long-distance routes, or GRP paths (*sentiers de Grande Randonnée de Pays*), are also to be found in the Cathar region. These are waymarked with small red and yellow painted rectangles.

The website of the FFRP, www.ffrp.asso.fr, and websites of the various regional and departmental branches of the FFRP (access to which can be gained from the main FFRP website), are good sources of information about long-distance paths in France. Others include www.gr-infos.com. The websites of various tourist agencies are also useful. For example, www.audetourisme.com has helpful information about long-distance paths in Aude.

Notes on Particular Long-distance Paths in the Cathar Region

The approximate routes of the national long-distance paths that cross Cathar castle country are described below. More information about the publications referred to can be found in Appendix 4.

The GR 107, le Chemin des Bonshommes, runs over the spine of the Pyrenees from Montségur southwards to Berga in Spain. It is said to follow a route taken by Cathars fleeing from persecution.

In Cathar castle country, the GR107 follows the Sentier Cathare from Montségur to Comus, then branches off southwards to Prades and Montaillou. It then descends into the Ariège Valley at Mérens-les-Vals, south of Ax-les-Thermes.

The GR107 is described in a detailed and interesting FFRP *topo-guide* entitled *Sur les traces des Cathares: le Chemin des Bonshommes* (ref: 1097). That guidebook also gives information about connecting links to Montségur from Foix and from Tarascon-sur-Ariège.

Relevant 1:25,000 maps for the GR107 in Cathar castle country are 2147ET (Foix), 2247OT (Lavelanet) and 2148ET (Ax-les-Thermes).

The GR7 runs from the Pyrenees, on the Andorra–France border, northeast and north across France to the Cévennes and to Dijon and Alsace. It enters Cathar castle country from the south, near Roc Blanc. There, it divides.

The main route, variously described as the GR7A or simply the GR7, heads north and eventually reaches Puivert. Staying on a roughly northward course, it then passes through Chalabre, Mirepoix and Fanjeaux. It crosses the Canal du Midi near Bram, then continues to head north.

The GR7B (also referred to as the GR7 bis) leaves the main GR7 route near Roc Blanc. It heads northwest to Montaillou, and near here joins the GR107 and the Sentier Cathare, coinciding with those trails as far as Montségur. The GR7B then turns northeast and rejoins the main GR7 route at Chalabre.

The *topo-guide* entitled *Traversée du Haut Languedoc* (ref: 716) describes the route of the GR7 north of near Bram. But the sections to the south – that is, in the Cathar region – are not yet the subject of a *topo-guide*.

Relevant 1:25,000 maps for the GR7 in Cathar castle country are 2248ET (Axat/Quérigut), 2247OT (Lavelanet), 2246O, 2246E, 2245E and 2245O.

The GR36 starts in the eastern Pyrenees and follows a roughly north-north-west line to cross the whole of mainland France, finishing on the Normandy coastline near Caen. It enters Cathar castle country from the south, after descending from the Canigou massif, then crosses the Fenouillèdes to Caudiès-de-Fenouillèdes. It then heads east as far as Peyrepertuse Castle. There, it turns resolutely to the north and crosses the Corbières region.

Deep in the Corbières hills, the GR36 divides. The main route (referred to variously as the GR36A or simply the GR36) goes north, passes by the ruins of the Cathar castle at Termes and follows a sinuous route north to Mayronnes. It then heads northeast to Lagrasse, where there is a fine Benedictine abbey.

The GR36B performs a loop to the east, heading for Villerouge-Termenès (where there is a well-preserved Cathar castle). At present the GR36B, between where it leaves the main GR36 and Villerouge-Termenès, is not shown on the 1:25,000 map (2447OT, Tuchan). However, it is waymarked on the ground. It leaves the main GR36 just south of Mouthoumet and passes through the villages of Laroque-de-Fa, Maisons and Palairac.

North of Villerouge-Termenès, the GR36B crosses the Serre de Blanes limestone plateau. It descends to St-Pierre-des-Champs, then climbs to meet the main GR36 path just west of Lagrasse.

There is a west–east link between the GR36A at Termes and the GR36B at Villerouge-Termenès. This link used to be part of the GR36B, but is now called the GR36AB. On the current 1:25,000 map, the GR36AB is still shown as the GR36B.

From Lagrasse, the GR36 climbs the Montagne d'Alaric and turns west to Carcassonne. After passing running through Carcassonne, it heads north to climb towards the Montagne Noire region.

Only the very southernmost part of the GR36 in Cathar castle country (that is, south from about Peyrepertuse Castle) is currently described in a published *topo-guide – La Traversée des Pyrénées, Pyrénées Orientales,* ref: 1092.

Relevant 1:25,000 maps for the GR36 in Cathar castle country are 2348ET (Prades), 2347OT (Quillan), 2447OT (Tuchan), 2446O, 2346E and 2345E.

The GR77 is a link between the GR36 and the GR7. It branches off from the GR36 north of Lagrasse, heads northeast to cross the Canal du Midi near Lézignan-Corbières, then continues roughly northwards to join the GR7 in the Haut Languedoc regional park.

The GR77 in Cathar castle country is not described in a published FFRP *topo-guide.*

Relevant 1:25,000 maps for the GR77 in the region are 2446O and 2445E.

The Canal du Midi towpath, which extends from Toulouse to Bram, Carcassonne then Béziers, is not an official long-distance path, but it is good for walking (and cycling) and is a *de facto* long-distance path. Its route is obvious.

Relevant 1:25,000 maps for the Canal du Midi in the Cathar region are 2224SO, 2245E, 2345O, 2345E, 2445O, 2445E, 2545O and 2545ET (Béziers).

Possible Walking Tours Using Long-distance Paths in the Cathar Region
If you are planning a walking tour in Cathar castle country of between a few days and three weeks, you could of course simply follow all or part of the Sentier Cathare, or one of the GR paths described above. But it is also possible to devise tours which use sections of more than one long-distance path, and which pass close to a number of Cathar sites and other places of exceptional interest. Tours of this kind, which start and finish in places accessible by public transport, include the following. Many others are of course possible.

1 A Tour of About Three Weeks (including travel to and from Britain)
Train/plane from Britain to Toulouse or Carcassonne; train/bus to Bram.
- South on GR7 via Fanjeaux (used as a base by Simon de Montfort, the crusade's military leader), Mirepoix (built since the Cathar period, but with a well-preserved medieval town centre), Chalabre, then on the GR7B to Montségur.
- East on the Sentier Cathare northern branch to Quillan via Puivert, with an optional day for a visit to Montaillou.
- Continue east on the Sentier Cathare to Peyrepertuse, with an optional day for an ascent of the Pech de Bugarach en route.
- One-day circuit on the Sentier Cathare from Peyrepertuse to Quéribus and back.
- North on GR36 from Peyrepertuse to Termes, then east on the GR36AB to Villerouge-Termenès.
- North on GR36B to Lagrasse, then west on GR36 to finish in Carcassonne.
- Train/plane from Carcassonne or Toulouse (train connection from Carcassonne) to Britain.

2 A Tour of About Two Weeks (including travel to and from Britain)
- Britain to Carcassonne by train/plane; south to Quillan by bus/train (about one hour by train from Carcassonne).
- Pick up the Sentier Cathare at Quillan, then head east as in Tour 1, going to Peyrepertuse, taking a day to go out and back to Quéribus, then heading north to end in Carcassonne.
- Plane/train back to Britain, as for Tour 1.

3 A Tour of About One Week (including travel to and from Britain)
- Britain to Foix by plane and/or train via Toulouse.
- Three days on the Sentier Cathare, east to Roquefixade, Montségur and Comus.
- One day south on the GR107, via Montaillou to Ax-les-Thermes.

- (**Note** The GR107 doesn't actually go through Ax-les-Thermes, but the latter can easily be reached by turning off the GR107 at Fournit Granges, just south of Ascou. From that point, turn right onto a local walking route that carries yellow waymarks and is signposted for Ax-les-Thermes. After about 40 minutes descent you arrive in the spa town, where you can reward your feet with a paddle in the hot water of the age-old Bassin des Ladres.)
- Ax-les-Thermes north to Foix by bus or train.

APPENDIX 4

Useful Publications

There is a huge amount of literature, in many languages, about Cathars, Cathar castles and walking in the Cathar region. Many English publications on these subjects are available in bookshops in Britain.

Useful relevant websites for purchasing publications include www.amazon.co.uk and www.fnac.com. Try also the addresses and websites referred to in the section in the introduction on maps (those of the IGN, Stanford's, and so on).

Many publications in French – walks guidebooks, general books, tourist guidebooks, special editions of glossy magazines, and so on – can be bought in bookshops (*libraries*) and newsagents' (*maisons de la presse*) in and around Cathar castle country. More and more publications in English are also being stocked in such outlets.

The publications listed below amount to only a tiny fraction of the relevant literature. They are mostly those that the author has found useful in preparing this book, and are worth recommending, but it is not suggested that they are necessarily the best of what is available.

There is a guidebook to the Cathar Way in French (*le Sentier Cathare*), published by Rando éditions. Its photographs and other illustrations of Cathar castles and the surrounding countryside are beautiful, and the sections in the book on the Cathars, the Inquisition, the individual castles and so forth are a mine of fascinating information. At the time of writing, the most recent edition was published in 2005, and seems to be available only in shops in France.

My earlier guidebook – *Walking in the Cathar Region* (Cicerone, 2005) – contains descriptions of several day-walks of different lengths. The walks have as their focal points Cathar castles or other locations associated with the Cathars. The order in which the walks are presented follows the sequence of events in the

13th century that led to the downfall of the Cathars. Their history is summarised in the book.

The relevant *topo-guides* for long-distance paths in the region that are published by the FFRP (whose address is in Appendix 6) are listed below. These *topo-guides* can be bought by credit card via, for example, the IGN and Stanford's websites, but not via the FFRP website.

Sur le Traces des Cathares, le Chemin des Bonshommes (FFRP topo-guide GR107, ref: 1097).

La Traversée des Pyrénées, Pyrénées Orientales (which includes a description of the GR36 south of near Peyrepertuse Castle, ref: 1092).

Traversée du Haut Languedoc (which contains a description of the GR7 north of near Bram, ref: 716).

A good general tourist guide in English to the part of France that includes Cathar castle country is *The Green Guide – Languedoc, Roussillon, Tarn Gorges*. It is published by Michelin Travel Publications.

Good books about the Cathars in English, aimed at the non-specialist reader and published relatively recently, include *The Perfect Heresy* by Stephen O'Shea (Profile Books), *The Yellow Cross – the story of the last Cathars, 1290–1329* by René Weis (Penguin) and *The Cathars – the most successful heresy of the Middle Ages* by Sean Martin (Pocket Essentials).

In French, the classic texts include *Histoire des Cathares* by Michel Roquebert (Perrin) and *Montaillou, Village Occitan* by Emmanuel Le Roy Ladurie (Gallimard). An English translation of the latter by Barbara Bray is entitled simply *Montaillou* (Penguin Books, 1978, reprinted 1990). Anne Brenon's *Petit Précis de Catharisme* (Loubatières) is an erudite but clear and succinct portrayal of the Cathars' beliefs, history and social context.

Succinct, too, is *The Land of the Cathars* by Georges Serrus (Loubatières). Translated from French, this is a richly illustrated glossy publication which describes each of the Cathar castles.

LISTING OF CICERONE GUIDES

IRELAND

The Mountains of Ireland
Irish Coastal Walks
The Irish Coast to Coast

INTERNATIONAL CYCLE GUIDES

The Way of St James – Le Puy to
  Santiago cyclist's guide
The Danube Cycle Way
Cycle Tours in Spain
Cycling the River Loire – The Way
  of St Martin
Cycle Touring in France
Cycling in the French Alps

WALKING AND TREKKING
IN THE ALPS

Grand Tour of Monte Rosa Vol 1
Grand Tour of Monte Rosa Vol 2
Walking in the Alps (all Alpine areas)
100 Hut Walks in the Alps
Chamonix to Zermatt
Tour of Mont Blanc
Alpine Ski Mountaineering
  Vol 1 Western Alps
Alpine Ski Mountaineering
  Vol 2 Eastern Alps
Snowshoeing: Techniques and Routes
  in the Western Alps
Alpine Points of View
Tour of the Matterhorn

FRANCE, BELGIUM AND
LUXEMBOURG

The Tour of the Queyras
Rock Climbs in the Verdon
RLS (Robert Louis Stevenson) Trail
Walks in Volcano Country
French Rock
Walking the French Gorges
Rock Climbs Belgium & Luxembourg
Tour of the Oisans: GR54
Walking in the Tarentaise and
  Beaufortain Alps
The Brittany Coastal Path
Walking in the Haute Savoie, vol. 1
Walking in the Haute Savoie, vol. 2
Tour of the Vanoise
Walking in the Languedoc
GR20 Corsica – The High Level Route
The Ecrins National Park
Walking the French Alps: GR5
Walking in the Cevennes
Vanoise Ski Touring
Walking in Provence
Walking on Corsica
Mont Blanc Walks
Walking in the Cathar region
  of south west France
Walking in the Dordogne
Trekking in the Vosges and Jura
The Cathar Way

PYRENEES AND FRANCE / SPAIN

Rock Climbs in the Pyrenees
Walks & Climbs in the Pyrenees
The GR10 Trail: Through the
  French Pyrenees
The Way of St James –
  Le Puy to the Pyrenees

The Way of St James –
  Pyrenees-Santiago-Finisterre
Through the Spanish Pyrenees GR11
The Pyrenees – World's Mountain
  Range Guide
The Pyrenean Haute Route
The Mountains of Andorra

SPAIN AND PORTUGAL

Picos de Europa – Walks & Climbs
The Mountains of Central Spain
Walking in Mallorca
Costa Blanca Walks Vol 1
Costa Blanca Walks Vol 2
Walking in Madeira
Via de la Plata (Seville To Santiago)
Walking in the Cordillera Cantabrica
Walking in the Canary Islands 1 West
Walking in the Canary Islands 2 East
Walking in the Sierra Nevada
Walking in the Algarve

SWITZERLAND

The Jura: Walking the High Route &
  Ski Traverses
Walking in Ticino, Switzerland
Central Switzerland –
  A Walker's Guide
The Bernese Alps
Walking in the Valais
Alpine Pass Route
Walks in the Engadine, Switzerland
Tour of the Jungfrau Region

GERMANY AND AUSTRIA

Klettersteig Scrambles in
  Northern Limestone Alps
King Ludwig Way
Walking in the Salzkammergut
Walking in the Black Forest
Walking in the Harz Mountains
Germany's Romantic Road
Mountain Walking in Austria
Walking the River Rhine Trail
Trekking in the Stubai Alps
Trekking in the Zillertal Alps

SCANDINAVIA

Walking In Norway
The Pilgrim Road to Nidaros
  (St Olav's Way)

EASTERN EUROPE

Trekking in the Caucausus
The High Tatras
The Mountains of Romania
Walking in Hungary

CROATIA AND SLOVENIA

Walks in the Julian Alps
Walking in Croatia

ITALY

Italian Rock
Walking in the Central Italian Alps
Central Apennines of Italy
Walking in Italy's Gran Paradiso
Long Distance Walks in Italy's Gran
  Paradiso
Walking in Sicily
Shorter Walks in the Dolomites
Treks in the Dolomites

Via Ferratas of the Italian
  Dolomites Vol 1
Via Ferratas of the Italian
  Dolomites Vol 2
Walking in the Dolomites
Walking in Tuscany
Trekking in the Apennines
Through the Italian Alps: the GTA

OTHER MEDITERRANEAN
COUNTRIES

The Mountains of Greece
Climbs & Treks in the Ala Dag
  (Turkey)
The Mountains of Turkey
Treks & Climbs Wadi Rum, Jordan
Jordan – Walks, Treks, Caves etc.
Crete – The White Mountains
Walking in Western Crete
Walking in Malta

AFRICA

Climbing in the Moroccan Anti-Atlas
Trekking in the Atlas Mountains
Kilimanjaro

NORTH AMERICA

The Grand Canyon &
  American South West
Walking in British Columbia
The John Muir Trail

SOUTH AMERICA

Aconcagua

HIMALAYAS – NEPAL, INDIA

Langtang, Gosainkund &
  Helambu: A Trekkers' Guide
Garhwal & Kumaon –
  A Trekkers' Guide
Kangchenjunga – A Trekkers' Guide
Manaslu – A Trekkers' Guide
Everest – A Trekkers' Guide
Annapurna – A Trekker's Guide
Bhutan – A Trekker's Guide

AUSTRALIA AND NEW ZEALAND

Classic Tramps in New Zealand

TECHNIQUES AND EDUCATION

The Adventure Alternative
Rope Techniques
Snow & Ice Techniques
Mountain Weather
Beyond Adventure
The Hillwalker's Manual
The Book of the Bivvy
Outdoor Photography
The Hillwalker's Guide to
  Mountaineering
Map and Compass

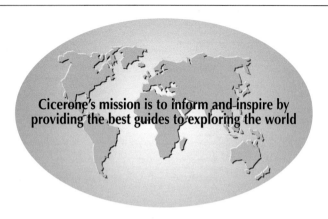

Cicerone's mission is to inform and inspire by providing the best guides to exploring the world

Since its foundation over 30 years ago, Cicerone has specialised in publishing guidebooks and has built a reputation for quality and reliability. It now publishes nearly 300 guides to the major destinations for outdoor enthusiasts, including Europe, UK and the rest of the world.

Written by leading and committed specialists, Cicerone guides are recognised as the most authoritative. They are full of information, maps and illustrations so that the user can plan and complete a successful and safe trip or expedition – be it a long face climb, a walk over Lakeland fells, an alpine traverse, a Himalayan trek or a ramble in the countryside.

With a thorough introduction to assist planning, clear diagrams, maps and colour photographs to illustrate the terrain and route, and accurate and detailed text, Cicerone guides are designed for ease of use and access to the information.

If the facts on the ground change, or there is any aspect of a guide that you think we can improve, we are always delighted to hear from you.

Cicerone Press
2 Police Square Milnthorpe Cumbria LA7 7PY
Tel:01539 562 069   Fax:01539 563 417
e-mail:info@cicerone.co.uk   web:www.cicerone.co.uk

CICERONE